American Mysticism
From William James to Zen

American
Mysticism
From William James to Zen

HAL BRIDGES

HARPER & ROW, PUBLISHERS
NEW YORK, EVANSTON AND LONDON

To Alice, Lois, and Stephanie

Contents

Preface

The title of this book, *American Mysticism: From William James to Zen*, is designed to indicate in a reasonably clear, concise, and evocative manner that the subject treated is mystical experience and thought in the United States since 1900. I do not mean to suggest that there is any such thing as a distinctively American form of mysticism. On the contrary, it seems to me that mysticism in America shows striking similarity to mystical patterns of experience and thought throughout the world's history. This view is explained in some detail in the introductory first chapter.

My interest in mystical literature goes back to 1949, when I first read Richard Maurice Bucke's *Cosmic Consciousness*. I began this study in the spring of 1963, after it occurred to me that I knew of no book entirely concerned with the history of mysticism in twentieth-century America. My approach to the subject is essentially that of the historian of ideas; but biographical inquiry into the lives of key mystics has also seemed essential, and I have paid some attention to mystical movements and the cultural impact of mysticism. I must emphasize, however, that I have not attempted definitive treatment of any person or topic, but rather an exploration of a relatively unknown field.

To guide the exploration, and with no thought whatever of saying the last word on subjects of extreme complexity, I offer in the first chapter my definitions of "mysticism," "mystical experience," and "mystic." The study concentrates upon the writings of outstanding and representative mystics, persons who have themselves had mystical experience; for I agree with Evelyn Underhill that it is the man crying "Oh, taste and see!" out of the conviction that he has tasted and seen who can best help us to understand mysticism.

The book is organized around the various frames of thought —for instance, the Judaeo-Christian tradition—within which these mystics have expressed themselves. The chapters form a broadly chronological pattern, moving from the early twentieth-century interests of William James to contemporary concern with Oriental mysticism. I hope that when the reader has finished the last chapter he will have experienced the pleasure that I have known along the way, and will agree with me that this unorthodox historical journey has been worthwhile.

Many kind persons have aided me in my work on this book, and though all cannot be named here I am grateful to each of them. My friend and colleague Edwin Scott Gaustad helped me clarify my views of mysticism and read most of the manuscript, to my great advantage. I much appreciate his generous assistance. Of course neither he nor anyone else mentioned here is responsible for my errors of fact or interpretation; these are mine alone.

Christopher Isherwood and Swami Prabhavananda read the manuscript chapter on Vedanta, and Prabhavananda provided the statements of his religious views that appear as Appendixes A and B. To these kind gentlemen I am very grateful.

Others whom I wish to thank for valuable advice and information provided at various stages of this project are Ralph H. Gabriel, Herbert Wallace Schneider, Howard H. Brinton, Allan Nevins, Abraham J. Heshel, John Tracy Ellis, Gerald Heard, Mia and Alex Lipski, Robert V. Hine, the late Philip Wheelwright, Patricia and John L. Beatty, Donald Lowe, George Bikle, Aileen Fisher, the late Olive Rabe, Joyce Lebra, Gladys Weibel, Martin Rist, Louise Black, Thérèse and Clifford P. Westermeier,

Marian McKenna, Edith Runyan, Joe Harris, Silas Hoadley, and Benjamin Saltman.

It is a pleasure to acknowledge assistance received from the University of California in the form of grants in aid of research and a Senior Faculty Fellowship. My thanks are also due the University of Colorado for a Faculty Fellowship. Librarians of the University of Colorado and of the University of California at Riverside, Berkeley, and Los Angeles have been unfailingly helpful. And through the years, the secretaries of the History Department at Riverside have cheerfully and accurately typed various drafts of the manuscript.

My wife, Alice, introduced me to mystical literature, encouraged me to begin and to finish this project, served as a discerning critic of the manuscript, and aided me in many other ways. I have tried to express in a measure my gratitude by dedicating the book to her, and to my daughters Lois and Stephanie, who have also been an inspiration.

Portions of Chapters 5 and 7 initially appeared in the *Journal of the American Academy of Religion* under the title "Aldous Huxley: Exponent of Mysticism in America," XXXVII (December, 1969).

University of California, Riverside   H.B.

CHAPTER 1

Ground for Exploration

Perennially, the world over, mysticism has been a means by which man has expressed his deepest thoughts and highest aspirations. Scholars have long recognized this fact, and have produced numerous historical studies of mysticism, investigating the ways in which it has entered into the intellectual tradition of many lands, from the Far East to the Western nations. The reader who is interested in the mystical heritage of a particular country can find historical monographs on the subject of mysticism in India, in England, Germany, France, Italy, Spain—the list extends through a considerable number of national categories. But it has never included the United States. The book now before you is, so far as I know, the first ever to be devoted entirely to the history of mysticism in America.[1] It explores one chronological segment of this relatively unknown historical ground, the period from 1900 to the present time.

During this period the American people, like those of other lands, have shown persistent interest in mysticism, an interest that may now be rising to an unprecedented peak. If the wave is in fact rising to new heights, its crest would seem to be the intensified popularity of Oriental mysticism that developed in America after the second world war and received renewed impetus in the fifties and sixties from the vogue for psychedelic drugs. Whether or not these drugs can produce mystical experience is a question that has aroused recent and continuing controversy. Knowledge of psychedelic agents, however, is not recent but very old, and we shall find experimentation with them in the early as well as the recent years of the twentieth century.

The word "mysticism," which is connected etymologically with the mystery rites of ancient Greece, has become a kind of catchall term for anything that seems mysterious or otherworldly. So loosely, indeed, is it often used that explicit statement of what it means for the purpose of this study is in order. I shall follow, in the main, three recognized authorities, Rufus M. Jones, Evelyn Underhill, and W. T. Stace, who have sought to clarify the meaning of mysticism and to write about it with a reasonable degree of precision.[2] These thoroughgoing investigators suggest, with other authorities, that mysticism is a recognizable pattern of experience and thought, discernible in the utterances of mystics throughout world history, notwithstanding the differences that prevail among them with regard to time and place and philosophical and religious beliefs. They further suggest that the core of mysticism is experience. As to the nature of that experience, let us see what some outstanding mystics have to say. Al-Ghazali (c. 1058–1111), most famous of the Sufis of Islam, writes as follows.

"The window into the unseen is opened in waking hours for the gnostic who has striven and is purified, being delivered from the power of sensual desire. Such a gnostic, sitting in solitude, who closes the channels of the senses, and opens the eye and ear of the spirit, and places his heart in relation with the Divine World, while he says continually: 'God, God, God' within his heart, not with his tongue, ceases to be aware of himself, and of this world, and remains seeing only Him Who is Most Glorious and Exalted."

This is a lucid description not only of mystical experience but also of the moral preparation and the meditation (hallmarks of the mystical life) that lead to it. Al-Ghazali further comments: "When the mystic enters into the pure and absolute Unicity of the One and into the Kingdom of the one and Alone, mortals reach the end of their ascent. . . . No higher ascent for the soul is possible, for there is no height beyond the highest and no multiplicity in the face of the Unity. . . ."[3]

Unity—Oneness—this quality of mystical experience is stressed again and again by the great mystics. Note how it is emphasized by the Neoplatonist philosopher Plotinus (*c.* 205–270) in this passage from his *Enneads.* "No doubt we should not speak of seeing; but we cannot help talking in dualities, seen and seer, instead of, boldly, the achievement of unity. In this seeing, we neither hold an object nor trace distinction; there is no two. The man is changed, no longer himself nor self-belonging; he is merged with the Supreme, sunken into it, one with it. . . ."[4]

We might note, too, that both Al-Ghazali and Plotinus seem to be describing direct experience in which the ordinary senses and the self, the ego, are somehow transcended. Similarly, the German theologian Meister Eckhart (1260–1328) speaks of the loss of self: "I say that if the soul is to know God, it must forget itself . . . for as long as it is self-aware and self-conscious, it will not see or be conscious of God. But when, for God's sake, it becomes unself-conscious and lets go of everything, it finds itself again in God. . . ."[5]

In each of the foregoing instances, the mystic seems to be looking inward, and there is no mention of objects in the outer world. But mystical experience may also involve outward vision. Eckhart declares, "All that a man has here externally in multiplicity is intrinsically One. Here all blades of grass, wood and stone, all things are one." And William Blake sings,

> To see a World in a Grain of Sand
> And a Heaven in a Wild Flower,
> Hold Infinity in the palm of your hand
> And Eternity in an hour.[6]

On the basis of such utterances, Stace and other authorities differentiate between what Stace terms "extrovertive" and "introvertive" mystical experiences, but it seems unnecessary for us to do so. The mystics themselves, as Stace remarks, generally

3

"do not distinguish between the introvertive One and the extro-vertive One."[7] Neither shall we attempt to make the distinction between "mild" and "extreme" mystical experience upon which James Bissett Pratt insists in his authoritative study, *The Religious Consciousness.*[8] Rather, as the mystics tend to do, we shall regard the inward and the outward, the mild and the extreme, as being all of one piece.

As anyone who cares to investigate mystical literature may determine for himself, the half-dozen examples of mystical statement that we have considered can be paralleled innumerable times with examples from the writings of scores of mystics, East and West; and while no mystic will be found to say exactly the same thing as any other, all will seem to be describing more or less the same kind of experience. This similarity of utterance, which in the words of William James "ought to make a critic stop and think," is the basis of the premise that mysticism is a recognizable pattern of experience and thought.

I shall now venture into definition, not because I entertain the fatuous notion of producing *the* definition of mysticism, but simply because any writer who deals at length with this subject must define his terms if his readers are to understand what he means when he uses them. It seems to me that if something of the essence of what the mystics tell us could be captured in a one-sentence definition, it might run somewhat like this: Mysticism is selfless, direct, transcendent, unitive experience of God or ultimate reality, and the experient's interpretation of that experience. This is what I shall mean whenever I use the term "mysticism," and from this definition two others follow. Always in this study the phrase "mystical experience" will mean selfless, direct, transcendent, unitive experience of God or ultimate reality. Always the term "mystic" will mean a person who has had mystical experience.

Let me emphasize that when we select mysticism as ground for historical exploration we are dealing not only with experience but also with thought. As we recognize in our definition of mysticism, the mystic makes others aware of his experience—

perhaps makes himself aware of it—by interpreting it. He first thinks about it, interpreting it to himself. Then he may tell others about it, and often he writes about it. Therefore the present study is to some extent a history of ideas. For the mystic interprets his mystical experience by means of ideas, which reflect his intellectual background—for instance, philosophy, or Quakerism, or perhaps Vedanta, or Zen Buddhism. Of course, a mystical idea may be an eclectic blend, drawn from various provinces of thought. And as we encounter it in the form, say, of theological speculation, or social criticism, or an incident in a novel, it may be not so much direct interpretation of personal mystical experience as thought which has merely been influenced by it, perhaps somewhat remotely.

The reader may feel that in attempting to devise a precise definition of mysticism I have sacrificed the rich texture of the living experience, and he will be right. Even the illustrative examples that led up to the definition were chosen more for their relative precision than for their emotional quality, yet strong emotion often characterizes mystical writings. Mystics frequently express feelings of the holy or the divine; of love, for God and fellow man and every living thing; of joy, and peace and tranquillity; of moral concern—the list could be lengthened. I do not suggest that we try to define mysticism in terms of such feelings. But by way of offsetting the dryness of definition let me call once more upon the great mystics. Here is St. Augustine (354–430), addressing his God of Love:

"I entered even into my inward self, Thou being my Guide: and able I was, for Thou wert become my Helper. And I entered and beheld with the eye of my soul . . . above my mind, the Light Unchangeable. . . . He that knows the Truth, knows what that Light is; and he that knows It, knows eternity. Love knoweth it. O Truth Who art Eternity! and Love Who art Truth! and Eternity Who art Love!"[9]

And here is Shankara (788–820), renowned mystic and foremost philosopher of India. "The ego has disappeared. I have realized my identity with Brahman, and so all my desires have melted away. I have risen above my ignorance and my knowledge of this seeming universe. What is this joy that I feel? Who shall measure it? I know nothing but joy, limitless, unbounded!"[10]

The Spanish Carmelite friar, St. John of the Cross (1542–1591), writes beautifully in poetry and prose of the peace and the "Divine tranquillity" of his mystical experience, explaining that "in this tranquillity the understanding sees itself raised up in a new and strange way, above all natural understanding, to the Divine light, much as one who, after a long sleep, opens his eyes to the light which he was not expecting."[11]

As for moral concern, Al-Ghazali has already spoken to us of the moral preparation that bulks so large in the mystical life. And St. Catherine of Genoa (1447–1510) exemplifies the reaction of many a Christian mystic who in the mirror of mystical experience has seen moral imperfections. "No more sins!" she cried, and entered at once upon the Purgative Way.[12]

Also reflected in these writings are other favorite themes of the mystics, such as inner light, the ultimate unreality of this world, the existence of a timeless realm of eternity, and the apprehension of mystical truth beyond reasoning—"above my mind," as St. Augustine says; "above all natural understanding," as St. John of the Cross expresses it. We shall find that mystics of twentieth-century America write in a similar vein, and that they hold the great mystics of world history in high regard.

Thus far, we have been largely concerned with what mysticism is; the other side of the coin is what it is not. From our definitions it follows that we cannot regard as mystics nor as mysticism many persons and things to which these terms are sometimes applied. Our definition of mysticism distinguishes it from magic, occultism, spiritualism, parapsychological phenomena, New Thought, and mental healing. It also distinguishes it from the thought of scientists like Albert Einstein who express reverence for the order of the universe; of philosophers and theologians like William Ernest Hocking and Paul Tillich who show varying degrees of sympathy toward mysticism as a way of knowledge;

and of literary artists like T. S. Eliot who employ mystical im-
agery as an esthetic means of communication. All these person-
ages and others like them have sometimes been labeled mystics,
but we shall not so regard them. Neither can we join hands with
those present-day philosophers who interpret mysticism in naturalistic terms and compare it with the existentialist nausea of
Jean-Paul Sartre.[13]

Additionally, we should note that the great mystics in general
and a number of leading authorities, including Jones, Underhill,
and Stace, agree that visions and voices should not be considered
important evidence of mystical experience. While mystics have
sometimes reported being subject to these phenomena, they
have cast much doubt on their significance, suggesting that the
higher forms of mystical experience, at any rate, are imageless
and soundless.[14] This attitude has not spared them the strictures
of psychologists. Sigmund Freud, in his *Civilization and Its Dis-
contents*, dismissed mysticism with a smile and a quotation from
Schiller, "Let him rejoice who breathes up here in the roseate
light!"[15]—while others have dwelt unsmilingly upon evidences
of hysteria in the extreme behavior that some of the famous
mystics have exhibited. Twentieth-century American mystics,
as we shall see, have understandably refused to regard mystical
experience as pathological, and on the contrary have argued that
it can enhance mental health.

In attempting to determine what is not mysticism and who is
not a mystic, I do not, of course, pretend to pass final judgments.
Nor do I claim that I have gathered into this book all figures of
twentieth-century America who are mystics by my definition.
Quite the contrary. This is not an exhaustive nor a definitive
study; it is an exploratory one. My intent is to point out some
of the more important and representative mystics in the period
since 1900 and to examine the mystical ideas that they have
expressed in their numerous books. These men are thinkers and
writers of a high order. Some, like Rufus Jones, Thomas Merton,
and Aldous Huxley, are exceptionally talented authors who have
reached international reading audiences. Their mystical experi-

ence and thought has not heretofore been drawn together and considered within the context of the world tradition of mysticism.

It is not my purpose to argue either for or against the beliefs of any of these individuals or of any person mentioned in this book. The most fruitful procedure for us to follow, I suggest, is to listen to the mystics with open-minded respect—"in the spirit of William James," to borrow a phrase from Ralph Barton Perry —as they tell us what they have experienced and how they interpret it, and what they think of the meaning of life and the problems of human existence. In the end, none of us will be likely to feel entirely uncritical, for mysticism in twentieth-century America encompasses much variety of faith and tradition. Some may end up as sharply censorious as George Santayana, who declared that "mysticism is the most primitive of feelings and only visits formed minds in moments of intellectual arrest and dissolution." Others, perhaps even those who remain as steadfast in their skepticism toward the mystical way of knowing as Bertrand Russell, may nevertheless conclude, like him, that mystical thinkers offer a special kind of wisdom, which should not be ignored.[16] Still others, sympathetic toward mysticism, may find in these pages fresh insights into their own deepest feelings and beliefs. All will agree, I hope, that some measure of historical light has been shed where it has long been needed.

As we examine the thought of these mystics of twentieth-century America, we shall find that often they seem remote from their time and place, detached to a marked degree from historical events. Politics, wars and threats of war, economic depression, industrialization and urbanization, atomic power, racial strife—the turbulent stream seems somehow to flow around and not through them. As men they may, of course, be actively concerned with such events; a number of them have been pacifists and social workers and one, Howard Thurman, is intimately involved in racial issues. But as mystical thinkers they tend to rise above the stream and view it from the perspective of eternity. Though occasionally their ideas may reflect the

pressing events of the day, more often they are intensely interested—as mystics the world over have always been interested—
in timeless questions of good and evil, of the nature of God or
ultimate reality, and of "the imprisoned splendor" within man
and how it may be found.

This may strike us as an incongruous way to think in a country
that has so often been characterized, especially by foreign travel-
ers, as the quintessence of materialistic practicality. Should
we then conclude that these mystics are simply exceptional
swimmers against the social current, "inner-directed"
men in the fullest sense of David Riesman's phrase? Or does
the fact that they have flourished as mystical thinkers in the
United States indicate that twentieth-century American civilization is more hospitable to mysticism than has been generally
realized? These are questions to which we shall return in the final
chapter.

Foremost among the intellectual influences that have helped
to shape the thinking of these mystics is the world tradition of
mysticism which I have already discussed. In one way or another
it has influenced every thinker whom we shall meet. A facet of
this world tradition is the American mystical heritage, encom-
passing such figures as Jonathan Edwards, Ralph Waldo Emerson, and Walt Whitman. Naturally enough, it has held more
interest for native American mystics than for those who have
immigrated to the United States.

Three other broad influences that should be mentioned at this
point are idealistic philosophy, evolutionary thought, and the
West's growing knowledge of Asian religions. Idealism, with its
thrust toward the spiritual and the monistic view of reality,
accords well with traditional mysticism; and from the last
decades of the nineteenth century onward countless American
college students have been taught idealistic forms of thought,
from Plato to Kant to Hegel and the post-Hegelians. For example, the Quaker mystic Rufus Jones received such training. So
also did John Wright Buckham, whose *Mysticism and Modern
Life* (1915) reveals what the author calls his "inward exhilara-

tions" and interprets mysticism from the viewpoint of personal idealism. This is not to suggest, however, that a philosophy so varied and widespread as idealism had to be learned in an American college classroom. Certainly immigrant mystics like Aldous Huxley did not learn it that way.

Evolutionary thought, which gained its scientific credentials in 1859 with the publication of Charles Darwin's *The Origin of Species*, has been an important factor in the molding of the modern psychology that twentieth-century mystics both utilize and defend themselves against. It also blends with mysticism in the form of hypotheses of emergent evolution, such as the one that Richard Maurice Bucke advanced in his *Cosmic Consciousness*, published in Philadelphia in 1901. Bucke told how, on one occasion, a "momentary lightning-flash of the Brahmic Splendor" gave him a "slight experience" of "cosmic consciousness," and argued that the human race, having evolved from "simple consciousness" to "self consciousness" was destined to continue evolving into cosmic consciousness, which an elite vanguard, including great religious leaders like Buddha, Jesus Christ, and Mohammed, had already attained.[17]

Like Darwinism, the modern expansion of the West's knowledge of Asian religions dates from the nineteenth century. When transcendentalist writers like Emerson and Thoreau read Hindu scriptures they were ahead of their time, but in the second half of the century the German philologist Max Müller pioneered in the systematic study of the world's religions that has ever since engaged increasing numbers of Western scholars. By 1939 a standard bibliography on Buddhism alone could list more than two thousand works in the English language. Growing knowledge of Asian religions has given intellectual impetus to the popular interest in Oriental mysticism that we have noticed, and has of course left its imprint on the minds of twentieth-century mystics concerned with Buddhism and Vedanta. It is also reflected in present-day writings on psychedelic experience. These often employ Oriental concepts.

But initially, when American philosophers reported and discussed psychedelic experience they drew not so much upon Oriental religion as upon German idealism. Their views of mysticism, and of experiments with psychedelic agents, are the subject of the next chapter.

CHAPTER 2

Experiments in Philosophy

In the spring of 1900, in a chateau on the French Mediterranean, an intense, gray-bearded gentleman lay propped up in bed, writing. Professor William James of Harvard, author of *The Principles of Psychology* and *The Will to Believe*, was on leave in Europe trying to recover from a strained heart. He was also slowly and painfully writing his Gifford Lectures on Natural Religion. Soon he would deliver them before large and appreciative audiences at the University of Edinburgh,[1] and in 1902 he would publish them as *The Varieties of Religious Experience.* Other, philosophically more impressive volumes on pragmatism, metaphysics, and epistemology would follow before his death in 1910. But none of his works would be more viable or better loved by successive generations than the *Varieties.* It made William James an authority on religion, including especially mystical experience, and for nearly seven decades his name has remained inseparably linked with mysticism in America.

Was James, then, a mystic? He himself said that he was not. In the *Varieties* he wrote of mystical states of consciousness, "my own constitution shuts me out from their enjoyment almost entirely, and I can speak of them only at second hand." In his private correspondence he remarked on more than one occasion that he had no mystical experience of his own, but just enough of the "germ" of mysticism in him to give him sympathy toward and some understanding of mystical states. That might seem to settle the question. But on the other hand no less an authority than Ralph Barton Perry has concluded in his monumental *Thought and Character of William James* that the great philosopher's statements to the contrary notwithstanding he did have infrequent experiences "of the type called mystical."[2] The most impressive evidence for this argument is found in a letter that James wrote to his wife on July 9, 1898, just after a hike in the Adirondack Mountains during which he had what he called a "most memorable" experience.

It occurred on Mt. Marcy, on a still, clear night while his companions lay sleeping. "I got into a state of spiritual alertness of the most vital description," he confided to Mrs. James, adding that he spent much of the night

in the woods, where the streaming moonlight lit up things in a magical checkered play, and it seemed as if the Gods of all the nature-mythologies were holding an indescribable meeting in my breast with the moral Gods of the inner life. . . . The intense significance of some sort, of the whole scene, if one could only *tell* the significance; the intense inhuman remoteness of its inner life, and yet the intense *appeal* of it; its everlasting freshness and its immemorial antiquity and decay; its utter Americanism, and every sort of patriotic suggestiveness, and you, and my relation to you part and parcel of it all, and beaten up with it, so that memory and sensation all whirled inexplicably together. . . . It was one of the happiest lonesome nights of my existence, and I understand now what a poet is. He is a person who can feel the immense complexity of influences that I felt, and make some partial tracks in them for verbal statement. In point of fact, I can't find a single word for all that significance, and don't know what it was significant of, so there it remains, a mere boulder of *impression*.[3]

James' biographer Gay Wilson Allen cites this interesting experience, as does Perry, and remarks that "in some respects it certainly was mystical."[4] There is no point in arguing that scholars should not use the term "mystical" broadly if they wish; many have done this, including James. Perhaps it is all the more significant, then, that he did not use the word in the description he wrote for his wife. And indeed he does not seem to be describing mystical experience as the term has been defined in the preceding chapter, for in his account he gives no indication of either selflessness, transcendence, or unity.

That he did not have mystical experience is further indicated by his treatment of it in his writings. In the *Varieties* he proposes "four marks which, when an experience has them, may justify us in calling it mystical for the purpose of the present lectures." These are (1) "ineffability"—the mystic, James points out, declares of his experience "that it defies expression, that no adequate report of its contents can be given in words"; (2) "noetic quality"—mystical experiences "are states of insight into depths of truth unplumbed by the discursive intellect"; (3) "transiency —mystical states cannot be sustained for long"; (4) "passivity" —during the experience "the mystic feels as if his own will were in abeyance, and indeed sometimes as if he were grasped and held by a superior power." While accurate enough, so far as they go, these marks are only relatively restrictive, and lead to James' application of the term "mystical" to a range of experience that seems excessively wide, since it includes such states of consciousness as "the deepened sense of the significance of a maxim or formula" and alcholic drunkenness. Moreover, he declares that "religious mysticism is only one half of mysticism," that the other half is found in "the text-books on insanity," and that paranoia, indeed, may be "a *diabolical* mysticism."[5] No mystic would use the terms "mystical" and "mysticism" so loosely. This treatment reveals not the man who knows by experience but the inquiring psychologist who would like to know; and plainly James is still inquiring in the article on "religious mysticism," published in 1910 in the *Journal of Philosophy*, in which he suggests that "states of mystical intuition may be only very sudden and great extensions of the ordinary 'field of consciousness.' "[6] In the light of all the evidence it seems more consistent to conclude that James was not a mystic.

Nevertheless, for two paramount reasons he is a figure of special significance to an understanding of mysticism in twentieth-century America. First, there is the influence of the *Varie-*

ties. Over and over again the book and its author have been cited in the writings of mystics. The philosophical prestige of James, his readability, the perceptiveness of his thought, the wealth of illustrative mysticism in his study—ranging from the poetry of Tennyson to the Vedanta philosophy of India and the works of the great Christian mystics—all this has drawn to the *Varieties* the person of mystical inclination. Nor should James' own inclination, his mystical "germ," be forgotten. For surely it is this that gives his book its atmosphere of warm sympathy toward mysticism. In it James writes of the "reality" and "paramount importance" of mystical states and declares that "mystical experiences are as direct perceptions of fact for those who have them as any sensations ever were for us." He also aligns mystical experience with the scientific thought of his day by drawing upon the developing psychological hypothesis of the subconscious and suggesting that mystical states "spring from the . . . great subliminal or transmarginal region." To be sure, he adds that both " 'seraph and snake' abide there," and that "to come from thence is no infallible credential." But on balance, despite the occasional doubts he raises, his treatment of mysticism is markedly favorable, and in the end he incorporates faith in the mystical outlook into his personal religious philosophy.[7] Indeed, in the *Varieties* he seems almost to yearn to *be* a mystic. If his head is not always for mysticism, his heart invariably is.

The second reason for the special significance of James is that he exemplifies, at the beginning of the twentieth century, the interest in psychedelic experience that has reached new heights in the fifties and sixties. James' interest seems to have been first aroused in 1874, when he reviewed for the *Atlantic Monthly* a privately printed pamphlet by Benjamin Paul Blood, *The Anaesthetic Revelation and the Gist of Philosophy,* in which Blood maintained that he had gained insight into "the genius of being" by taking anesthetics in experiments extending over nearly fourteen years. The review mixed caution with approval. Though James was "more than skeptical of the importance of Mr. Blood's so-called discovery," the "duty of the intellect" toward a man's "mystical experience," he suggested, "is not suppression but interpretation." He considered Blood's own interpretation "deficient," but had kind words for his style and his general philosophical observations. He also warned, in words that would be echoed years later by other critics of psychedelic experimentation, "What blunts the mind and weakens the will is no full channel for truth, even if it assist us to a view of a certain aspect of it. . . ."[8]

This cautionary attitude did not prevent James from striking up a friendly correspondence with Blood, nor from trying anesthesia on himself. In the early 1880's he experimented with nitrous oxide. The initial "keynote" of his experience, as he afterward described it, was "the tremendously exciting sense of an intense metaphysical illumination," in which "the ego and its objects . . . are one." But as the effects of the gas wore off the "feeling of insight" faded, and James decided that he had not discovered anything of great importance. Even more unsatisfactory was his experiment in 1896 with the psychedelic properties of mescal cactus. The United States Government had distributed a supply of peyote buttons to certain medical men, including S. Weir Mitchell, who sent some to James. The peyote had given Mitchell visions of jewellike color. One button made James, as he wrote his brother Henry, "violently sick for 24 hours." He had "no other symptom whatever" except a hangover the next day. "I will take the visions on trust!" he told Henry.[9]

Understandably, in the *Varieties* he did not mention his peyote experience. But he did write at some length of "mystical states" produced not only by alcohol but also by nitrous oxide, ether, and chloroform. In discussing nitrous oxide he quoted from Blood's *Anaesthetic Revelation* and mentioned his own experiences with the gas, taking a more positive view of what he had discovered than he had initially expressed. "One conclusion was forced upon my mind at that time," he said, "and my impression of its truth has ever since remained unshaken. It is that our normal waking consciousness, rational consciousness as we call it, is but one special type of consciousness, whilst all about

16

it, parted from it by the filmiest of screens, there lie potential forms of consciousness entirely different." Yet he was not certain "how to regard" his experiences. In retrospect he felt that "they all converge towards a kind of insight to which I cannot help ascribing some metaphysical significance. The keynote of it is invariably a reconciliation. It is as if the opposites of the world, whose contradictoriness and conflict make all our difficulties and troubles, were melted into unity." That this "monistic insight" accorded with Blood's, James pointed out. Nevertheless, at the end of the *Varieties* he turned away from monism toward "the pluralistic hypothesis,"[10] thus holding to a doctrine of *The Will to Believe* and foreshadowing his later work, *A Pluralistic Universe.*

If James was uncertain about the significance of his anesthetic insight, quite the opposite was true of Blood. Not the slightest doubt as to the overwhelming importance of the revelation that had come to him seemed ever to disturb this "unacademic philosopher"—to use Perry's phrase—who lived as a gentleman farmer on an inherited estate in Amsterdam, New York, and published essays on metaphysics in local newspapers. As a philosopher he had some dialectical skill and a flair for the striking phrase. But it is not likely that his name would have become widely known outside Amsterdam had he not advanced his claim that anesthesia opens the door to truth. Inquiring minds of the nineteenth century were intrigued by anesthetic experimentation. As early as 1800 Sir Humphrey Davy had experimented with nitrous oxide. Blood's *Anaesthetic Revelation*, which he printed and distributed at his own expense, brought him letters from a number of eminent men, including Tennyson, Sir William Ramsay, Emerson, and William James.[11]

James remarked of *The Anaesthetic Revelation* that it began "with dialectic reasoning, of an extremely Fichtean and Hegelian type," and ended "in a trumpet-blast of oracular mysticism."[12] The dialectic took up most of the essay but, paradoxically, Blood wrote philosophy in order to condemn it. In its place he offered the anesthetic pathway to truth.

After experiments ranging over nearly fourteen years I affirm—what any man may prove at will—that there is an invariable and reliable condition (or uncondition) ensuing about the instant of recall from anaesthetic stupor to sensible observation, or "coming to," in which the genius of being is revealed; but because it cannot be remembered in the normal condition it is lost altogether through the infrequency of anaesthetic treatment in any individual's case ordinarily, and buried, amid the hum of returning common sense, under that epitaph of all illumination: "this is a queer world."

The "central point of the illumination," he continued, was that

sanity is not the basic quality of intelligence . . . the naked life is realized only outside of sanity altogether; and it is the instant contrast of this "tasteless water of souls" with formal thought as we "come to," that leaves in the patient an astonishment that the awful mystery of Life is at last but a homely and a common thing, and that aside from mere formality the majestic and the absurd are of equal dignity. The astonishment is aggravated as at a thing of course, missed by sanity in overstepping, as . . . in making in the dark a step higher than the stair.

Although there was "a sadness in the tenor of the mystery," there was also "serenity and ancient peace," and "majesty and supremacy unspeakable." By means of the anesthetic revelation "we enter to the sadness and the majesty of Jesus—to the solemn mystery which inspired the prophets of every generation. By some accident of being they entered to this condition." And they had discovered what Blood now proclaimed, that ultimate reality is "the One," that "each is all, in God," and that "the kingdom of God is . . . within you; it is the Soul."[13]

The clear monistic note in this trumpet-blast of 1874 became in time so muted that it was barely audible. As the years passed and Blood worked under James' tutelage to achieve a fuller expression of his philosophy, he moved away from monism toward Jamesian metaphysics. Not until 1920 did the book that he projected as the culmination of his thought appear. It bore the title, *Pluriverse: An Essay in the Philosophy of Pluralism.*

It was in some respects an ambivalent and ambiguous work. In keeping with the title, and perhaps with the spirit of James peering over his shoulder, Blood resolutely argued against the

18

One, and called for "gods and gods in the 'lower cases.' " Yet, when as of old he invoked the anesthetic revelation as being more authoritative than philosophy, he expressed the hope "that the fond monism that we have dialectically disparaged may be at least transcendentally and mystically rehabilitated." The religious glow of his earlier references to the revelation had faded. He now stressed its secular quality, and the sense of "reminiscence of the *immemorial*" that it brought. Actually, it remained for him essentially inexpressible, and he confessed in the end that he could not really put into words what he had discovered. To keep asking him what his revelation was, he plaintively suggested, was "in bad form—a kind of counting of the spoons."[14] Though *Pluriverse* was not the book he had once hoped to write, it was the best he could do.

Many a mystic, of course, has failed to catch ineffability in a verbal net. But was Blood a mystic? Because of the possibility that he may have been, his thought has here been briefly considered. Yet one may wonder whether Blood really derived mystical experience from his experiments with "anaesthetic agents," by which unexplained term, judging from his friend James' remarks, he apparently meant nitrous oxide and ether. Granted that he made his claim honestly, he still could have been mistaken. The basic question is: can chemical agents induce mystical experience? It is so closely related to the present-day question—Can psychedelic drugs induce mystical experience?—that the two may best be considered together. For this reason, further discussion will be postponed until the arguments and evidence regarding psychedelic drugs can also be examined, in Chapter 7.

Another philosopher who has been generally regarded as a mystic, although he did not provide direct testimony of his personal mystical experience, is Charles A. Bennett, author of *A Philosophical Study of Mysticism* (1923) and *The Dilemma of Religious Knowledge* (1931). A native of Ireland, Bennett was educated in England at Trent College, Derbyshire, and Queen's College, Oxford. He came to America in 1909 and took his doctor's degree at Yale University, where he remained to teach, eventually becoming Professor of Philosophy. William Ernest Hocking, first his teacher and then his colleague at Yale, described him as "a notably successful teacher," as "a happy man" despite the suffering his almost constant ill health caused him, and as "a thinker who could *see.*"[15] After his death on May 1, 1930, at the age of forty-four, his *Philosophical Study* was reprinted by the Yale University Press with a preface by the well-known Quaker mystic, Rufus M. Jones, who recalled "the profound satisfaction" he had felt in 1923 on reading the book for the first time. "I knew at once as I read the chapters," he said, "that another interpreter of mysticism had come who could speak with authority and not alone from citations." Bennett was "a glowing illustration of his own claim that a mystic comes back from his experience of God 'with an invigorated grasp' upon the manifold interests of life."[16]

The view that Bennett was a mystic is borne out by both of his books. In *The Dilemma of Religious Knowledge* he argues for the supernatural element in religion, asserts that "the claim of religion to convey insight about the real world may not be denied," and makes it clear that he sympathizes with mystical insight.[17] But these posthumously published lectures deal with much else besides mysticism, and the fullest statement of Bennett's mystical ideas remains his *Philosophical Study.*

His concern in the study is "with mysticism as a way of life, in which the conspicuous element is the immediate experience of God." The "authentic mystic," he writes, is distinguished by his "genius for religious experimentation" and his "moral stamina." The latter trait, especially, marks him off from the merely abnormal or pathological type of personality with which some psychologists have sought to group him. For though the mystic often exhibits in his life mental phenomena that appear on the surface to be pathological, he is not at their mercy as is the person who is really mentally ill. The mystic "realises what is happening to him. He is self-conscious enough to ask what these things may mean. He has the character and the fixity of purpose to strive for the organisation of his inner life and in this struggle to make use of, and so to rise superior to, the accidents that befall him on his spiritual pilgrimage."

He persists in this pilgrimage not because he wants to solve philosophical problems, or to escape from the world and his personal difficulties, or to benefit himself in any way. What he desires is to become "one with God." And "God is not thought of as a director whose guidance is to be used in the conduct of life: He is not means but end; He is not used but loved."[18]

Clearly, to Bennett the moral quality in mysticism is of great importance. To be sure, he argues that morality can easily become too strenuous, and that it is not, alone, "a sufficient substitute for religion."[19] But he emphasizes that as an ingredient of the mystical life it is essential.

Consider, for instance, how mystics prepare themselves for their ineffable experience. "We miss the essence of the mystics' preparation," says Bennett, "unless we see that it is a *moral* preparation. They know that in order to see God one must be pure in heart and that there is some moral necessity in the divine response. They can never be sure that God will or must reveal himself to the waiting soul—the ultimate revelation is always by virtue of the grace of God; but they know, negatively, that without this moral preparation the vision will not be granted."

Again, because the divine response waits upon preparation of "the moral will," the seeker who neglects that preparation cannot discover mystical truth. Violence, magic—these will not avail him. In illustration of this argument Bennett evokes the shade of Benjamin Paul Blood.

You have heard, let us say, of the anaesthetic revelation. In the hope of gaining an intellectual illumination you inhale nitrous oxide gas. Revelation, of a sort, comes. That is not response; it is not even espionage; it is magic. You discover no connection between your experiment and its result, between doing something to your body and receiving something into your mind. Indeed, you do not really receive it into your mind at all, because your mind was precisely what was not prepared to receive it. And this is proved by the fact that, whatever certainties may be vouchsafed to you in the revelation, you cannot retain them after-wards.[20]

Enter one debit against psychedelic experience! But Aldous Huxley and others will have different views, and the ledger must be kept open.

When the seeker has made proper moral preparation and be-come a true mystic by achieving oneness with God, or "union with reality," as Bennett also terms it, he is ready to face the evil of the world with optimism. He can do this, says Bennett, be-cause the God with whom he has become united "is in the world reconciling it unto Himself. Here is the ground of his assurance. The mystic alone can read the black book of pessimism to the end . . . and still retain the militant address towards evil, because he is the conscious ally of that by which the evil may be con-quered."[21]

But, the pessimist might counter, has this optimistic seeker really found God, or is he merely indulging in self-delusion? Without going deeply into the question, Bennett upholds the validity of the mystical revelation. Though he notes that the utterances of mystics are not free from mistakes and exaggera-tions, and that they sometimes conflict with each other, he feels that this "need not wholly impair their truth. The mystic seeks the one God, the Substance of things, and says that he has found Him. He has a right to his certainty."

He also has a right to ask the philosopher to take him seri-ously, but not the right to replace the philosopher entirely. Both mysticism and philosophy are necessary, argues Bennett. The mystic is the miner producing old yet ever-new ore; the philoso-pher functions as its refiner; and both are responsible for the final product. Yet it should be remembered that "in the beginning was the ore." To Bennett it is mysticism that "seems . . . to have priority."[22]

Even as he expressed this view, he was well aware that it clashed with the temper of his times, and that in the America of the 1920's "our love of action, our naturalism, our secularism" were creating "an atmosphere in which the mystic cannot breathe."[23] Philosophy, he knew, was permeated by this atmosphere; the trend was away from speculative metaphysics and mysticism. It was a durable trend, which has run with increasing force and dominance into the 1960's. And yet it would be a rash prophet who would predict that America will never again have a mystical philosopher like Charles Bennett. For the wisdom of William James still applies. "Philosophy lives in words, but truth and fact well up into our lives in ways that exceed verbal formulation."[24]

CHAPTER 3

Quaker Lights

Although the "Mysticism" chapter in the *Varieties* evinces both the brilliance and the catholicity of the mind of William James, it omits discussion of an important group—the Society of Friends, or Quakers. James touches upon the Quakers elsewhere in the book, but overlooks them as exemplars of mysticism. Yet, at the time he wrote, they had been seeking and advocating the "Inner Light" in England and America for some two and a half centuries.

The early Quaker missionaries who brought George Fox's doctrines to America carried little theology. They were universalists who taught that the one God of mercy and love bestows some measure of the Inner Light—Himself as Father, Son (the Christ), or Holy Spirit—upon all men. Unregenerate man achieves spiritual regeneration by meditating upon the Light; this meditation is best practiced in a small group of believers. When they rightly "wait upon the Lord," they will be fused together into mystical Oneness with the divine Presence, as were the early Christians at Pentecost.

Thus a distinctive aspect of the original Quaker faith was group mysticism. In time, the Society of Friends experienced various divisions and secularizing influences.[1] But the mystical strain has persisted, in some branches more strongly than in others; and through the centuries it has produced some notable

American mystics. The eighteenth century had its John Woolman. The twentieth had Rufus Matthew Jones, editor, professor
of philosophy and ethics at Haverford College, humanitarian,
Quaker leader, and author of fifty-four books, popular and scholarly, on religious and mystical themes.

"Rufus Jones may undoubtedly be considered the most eminent American mystic of recent times, if, in fact, he is not the
American mystic *par excellence*," said Henry Nelson Wieman
and Bernard Eugene Meland in 1936, in their *American Philosophies of Religion*. "He has been in continuous association with
the eminent European mystics of our day," they added, "and his
publications through the years have been veritable gems of mystical insight, widely read and as widely appreciated." Interna-
tionally they placed him among "the greatest Christian mystics
of our time," with W. R. Inge and Underhill of England and
Rudolf Otto of Germany.[2]

Jones himself wrote frankly and engagingly on "Why I Enroll
with the Mystics." He was born with a pious bent, he said, into
a family of devout Maine Quakers, and his life and thought were
shaped by religious relatives, teachers, and friends. In boyhood
there was his saintly Aunt Peace. During his college years at
Haverford there was Professor Pliny E. Chase, who led him to
read Emerson and Carlyle and to write his graduating thesis on
mystics. Later there was his intimate Quaker friend John Wilhelm Rowntree of York, England, who was "essentially a mystic." And during a year of graduate study abroad there were
scholarly authorities at the universities of Heidelberg and Stras-
bourg who guided his work in his chosen specialties, philosophy
and mysticism.

In philosophy, he recalled, he became "deeply interested in
the Neo-Hegelian position especially as interpreted by Edward
and John Caird." He visited Edward Caird at Oxford. Nor did
he overlook that staunch anti-Hegelian, William James. Discov-
ering that James "was at work on the nature of mystical experience for his Edinburgh Gifford Lectures," he began to consult
with him. "It was always amazing the way this busy man wel-

25

comed a young quester," he later wrote. "Though never a disciple of his and though never able to accept in anything like fullness his central positions, I always felt that he gave me the stimulus of his friendship and I acknowledge . . . the immense debt I owe him."

Stronger influences were James' colleagues George Herbert Palmer and Josiah Royce, under whom Jones studied idealistic philosophy during a graduate year at Harvard, 1900–1901, when James happened to be on leave. As Jones remembered, Palmer "helped me to lay the foundations of my ethical theories," while Royce "had a larger influence on my intellectual development, I think, than any other one person." What inspired him most was Royce's concern with mysticism. "He took a group of us through his Aberdeen Gifford Lectures— *The World and the Individual* —and in that process we came to grips with his profound treatment of mysticism as one of the major pathways to reality. His treatment of mystical experience has always seemed to me of unusual value and I have greatly profited by his searching criticisms."[3] The last phrase was perhaps as near as sanguine Rufus Jones could come to admitting that in *The World and the Individual* Royce examines mysticism only to reject it.

For Jones mystical experience was infinitely more than a philosophical subject; it was the dominant fact of his life. At Quaker meetings he had many "experiences of communal worship in which the two worlds—the temporal and eternal—seem to fuse into one single world." He also had solitary mystical experiences, three of which seemed to him of paramount importance. The first occurred during his year abroad after graduation. "It was at Dieu-le-fit in France, near the foot-hills of the Alps," he recalled.

I was walking alone in a forest, trying to map out my plan of life and confronted with issues which seemed too complex and difficult for my mind to solve. Suddenly I felt the walls between the visible and the invisible grow thin and the Eternal seemed to break through into the world where I was. I saw no flood of light, I heard no voice, but I felt as though I were face to face with a higher order of reality than that of the trees or mountains. I went down on my knees there in the woods with that same feeling of awe which compelled men in earlier times to take off their shoes from their feet. A sense of mission broke in on me and I felt that I was being called to a well-defined task of life to which I then and there dedicated myself.[4]

In another account of this experience he wrote more explicitly of the sense of mission,

I saw stretch before me an unfolding of labor in the realm of mystical religion, almost as clearly as Francis heard himself called at St. Damiens to "repair the Church." I remember kneeling down alone in a beautiful forest glade and dedicating myself then and there in the quiet and silence, but in the presence of an invading Life, to the work of interpreting the deeper nature of the soul and its relation with God.[5]

The second experience came to him at the age of forty, aboard ship, near the end of a voyage to England. "Once at sea," he wrote of it, "in the middle of the night, when all unknown to me my little boy, left behind in America, was dying with no father by him to hold his hand, I suddenly felt myself surrounded by an enfolding Presence and held as though by invisible Arms. My entire being was fortified and I was inwardly prepared to meet the message of sorrow which was awaiting me next day at the dock."

After this moving event nearly two decades passed, and then on November 30, 1922, the third experience began when Jones, walking hurriedly across a road, was hit by an automobile. He had not seen it at all and was totally unprepared for what happened. "Suddenly I felt my chest break and cave in. At the same time there was a powerful impact on my leg and then my body was hurled through space with tremendous force. The odd thing was that I did no thinking. I just *felt*. I was vaguely aware that an irresistible force was crushing the life out of my body, but I had no touch of fear. . . . When the doctor arrived a few minutes after the accident, my heart was beating regularly and my pulse was normal." He had been thrown twenty feet. He had three broken ribs, torn ligaments, a fractured leg, an injured knee. But soon he resumed his college teaching, lecturing to his students in his home while lying flat on his back in a hospital bed in his library, bandaged and braced against the slightest movement, "feeling all the time," as he later said, "an unusual *élan.*" He marveled at the way the body can heal itself, and gradually it dawned upon him that

a "restoration" of another sort had gone on. I seemed in a new way to be liberated from fears and anxieties and worries. I had entered into an unexpected tranquility and peace. More than that I had gained an immense increase of vitality and *vis viva.* Life had become a more joyous and radiant affair than I had ever known. I no longer cared anything about arguments to prove the reality of God, any more than I did to prove the incomparable worth of the human love which surrounded my life as I lay quietly recovering. I do not know how I reached the new level of conviction or how I got from one stage of life to the higher one on which I found myself. It has always seemed to me to be a case of quiet mystical receptivity. Spiritual energies of a more or less permanent order flowed in and operated, as though God at my fountains far off had been raining.[6]

Such were the personal experiences that underlay the religious thought of Rufus Jones. In his numerous books, from his first mature statement, *Social Law in the Spiritual World* (1904) to the little volume *A Call to What Is Vital,* published in 1948, the year of his death, he held steadily to the goal of "interpreting the deeper nature of the soul and its relation with God" that had arisen before him at Dieu-le-fit. Specifically, he sought to interpret mysticism. In such works as *Studies in Mystical Religion* (1909) and *Spiritual Reformers in the Sixteenth and Seventeenth Centuries* (1914) he placed Quaker mysticism within a broad historical framework and earned a reputation as an outstanding writer of historical theology. In his autobiographical writings, and in unsystematic, urbanely persuasive expositions of his religious philosophy, of which *Social Law, Pathways to the Reality of God* (1931), and *The Testimony of the Soul* (1936) are among the best, he further examined the validity of the mystical experience and the role of the mystic in Christianity. Early in the century the London *Times* called him and William James the "two best stylists writing in America today." In 1945 Aldous

Huxley thanked him for "the much profit I have derived from your books."[7]

These works set forth mystical ideas that bear the triple stamp of Jones' personal experience, scholarly studies, and Quaker beliefs. His definitions of mysticism, though differing somewhat from one book to another, are essentially variations of his most precise formulation, which he first submitted in *Studies in Mystical Religion* and repeated in *The Luminous Trail* (1947): "Mysticism is the type of religion which puts the emphasis on immediate awareness of relation with God, on direct and intimate consciousness of the Divine presence. It is religion in its most acute, intense and living stage."[8]

By thus identifying mysticism with religion, he broke with William James' distinction between religious and nonreligious types. His psychological explanation of mystical consciousness, however, owed much to the *Varieties*, at least initially, when in *Social Law* he devoted a chapter to "the vast realm of the subconscious which, for all we know, borders upon the infinite Life, *rises out of it*, and may receive 'incursions' from it." Later he came to feel that James had led him to overemphasize "man's subliminal life," and by the mid-thirties he was ready to take a jocular view of the once-fascinating theory. "Those of us who were young at the time when the new wave of psychology swept over the modern world a generation ago believed that we were on the frontiers of new realms of life and thought about to be explored," he recalled. Expectantly they had waited "for the latest news which the psychologists were sure to bring us about the unfathomable reaches of the soul." But the psychologists discovered no soul, only mental phenomena. Some of then, "like . . . William James, did try to comfort us with the suggestion that the mind has a deep subcellar below the footlights of consciousness, where mysterious events might happen, a subliminal zone in which the bubbling springs of religion might well be allowed to bubble. . . . But it did not take very long to discover that the subliminal zone, like subtropical ones, had hissing serpents as well as glorious birds of paradise."

Serpents, and worse, as amply demonstrated by Freud and Jung. Of Jung's *Modern Man in Search of a Soul* Jones remarked, "This book does not give the modern man much light on how or where he is to find a soul." It merely afforded him "peeps" into the " 'dirt and darkness and evil' " of the unconscious. As for Freud, "it must be said in all fairness" that he "brought healing to many distraught persons. . . . But it can be just as certainly said that his conception of human life is repulsive and distorted and that his account of man's *psyche*, both above and below the threshold of consciousness, is a Freudian construction, not *homo sapiens* as he truly and really is."[9]

To Jones the psyche was not Freudian but spiritual; the soul was real. If it could not be found in James' subliminal zone, and certainly not in the Freudian unconscious—no matter. The mystic finds it where psychology cannot penetrate, and he knows that the soul stands on divine ground, that man is "a *finite-infinite being*," that "at our best we seem to be inwardly *conjunct* with the Life that is our Source. We find ourselves in intimate reciprocal relations with the ultimate Spiritual Reality of the universe. . . ."[10]

Jones rejected as "this new dogmatism" the contention of Barthian theologians that God is utterly unknowable, " 'an absolute Other.' " Mystics throughout history, he argued, have testified that God is immanent as well as transcendent, and that man can have "genuine fellowship and friendship with Him." This is corroborated by the New Testament, which reveals God as the loving Father. "He is essentially *Love—Agape*. . . . *Agape* is a unique type of Love, a Love that pours itself out regardless of merit, or desert—it floods out like the sun to reach the just and the unjust."[11]

Historically the one God of love, of infinite grace, has revealed Himself in the person of Christ. "Christ is this amazing grace of God made vocal and incarnate." Like other Quaker thinkers, Jones held that Jesus Christ was both completely human and completely divine, God's consummate revelation of Himself to the world. But he did not, like some Quakers of his day, speak of the Inner Light as the "Christ Within." When he referred to God in man he used such terms as "Presence," "Holy Spirit," and Emil Boutroux's "the Beyond that is Within." In summing up his mystical views of the divine-human relationship he pictured men as capable, through their free will, of controlling their own destiny, and of cooperating with God to form "the growing Kingdom of the spiritual Life." God, he declared, "finds His complete Life in and through us as we find ours in and through Him and through each other in love and joy and coöperation . . . . The Spiritual Universe is thus a concrete reality, not an abstract one, and the Life of God can be revealed and has been actually revealed in a temporal life set in the midst of time, in the Christ of Galilee and Judea and in and through Christian History, in raised and transformed lives, lived through His power, and . . . in the moral victories and demonstrations of the historical process."[12]

Thus Jones' idealistic religious philosophy envisioned a cosmos in which there was no cleavage between God and man. The inner world fit the outer as the hand the glove; rational man transcended time and space through such "spiritual values" as beauty, moral sentiments, and "a sense of Presence." These values, Jones argued, could not be reduced to the "fact-descriptions" of science, and psychology in particular should recognize the limits of its method. When James H. Leuba published his *Psychology of Religious Mysticism* (1926), in which he concluded that yogins, drug-users, and "the classical Christian mystics" were all alike mere victims of pathetic "self-deception," Jones retorted in his *New Studies in Mystical Religion* (1927) that the spiritual values, including mystical experience, occupied metaphysical ground beyond psychology's domain. "Psychology as an empirical science does not profess to deal, or at least ought not to profess to deal, with ultimate questions."[13] Leuba also concluded that "St Catherine of Genoa, Santa Theresa, Mme Guyon and St Marguerite Marie suffered from hysterical attacks," and he compared religious ecstasy to epilepsy. Jones as early as 1909 in his *Studies in Mystical Religion* had recognized

31

but somewhat discounted the element of hysteria in mysticism, and now in *New Studies* he admitted, "Nobody can read the lives of St. Francis of Assisi, St. Catherine of Genoa, Jacob Boehme, George Fox, Madame Guyon, or St. Teresa without feeling that these extraordinary persons had crises of illness which threatened to shatter both their physical and mental health. . . ." Still he objected to "the attack of the psychologist" on "the validity of mysticism." Some theorists, he declared, had reached the premature psychoanalytical conclusion that "religion is essentially a mild form of mental disease;" and that would mean that all mankind is more or less abnormal, a proposition he sharply rejected. "Some psychologists need psychotherapeutic treatment as much as some of our religionists do!"[14]

But the vexing question could not be completely dismissed. In 1939, when he published the last of his historical studies, *The Flowering of Mysticism*, he stated that through the years he had come to give greater weight than he had initially to the "large pathological factor" in the "lives of many mystics." It seemed to him that while mental instability was sometimes coupled with genius, leading to religious discovery which "in some notable instances" generated renewed health and increased spiritual power, it was too often not an asset for mystics but a persistent handicap. After all, health rather than disease was the highway to truth.[15]

But even though the mystic might not be suffering from mental disease, how could he refute the charge of self-deception, how validate his claim that what he experienced was the Holy Spirit? Jones could and did compare the mystical experience to the "sudden flashes of intuition" by which geniuses like Newton and Einstein sometimes made scientific discoveries, but he knew well enough that the mystic cannot demonstrate the objective reality of his insight in a mathematical equation. Indeed he readily admitted that for mystical experience "the usual verifications of our sense facts are wanting. The mystic cannot describe his object in the categories of common speech, nor can he get the corroborative testimony of other spectators. He has seen what he has seen, and in its first-hand quality of acquaintance it forever remains just his incommunicable experience. That seems, no doubt, a damaging admission and, for some, ends the debate." But Jones advanced the philosophical argument that values like beauty and obligation are in some sense objective, and averred that "there is the same kind of objective evidence in the highest forms of mystical experience." Certainly such experience carries with it "a majestic *conviction of objectivity.*" The mystic knows that he has reached divine ground just as the mountain climber knows that he has scaled his peak. "The sight itself is convincing." Or, put differently, "the experience of God which surges into the mystic's consciousness seems to him its own evidence of God." "For one who has the experience it has the same evidence that love ever has—the evidence of recognition and response." Finally, and most important, there is the evidence of results. The individual who has true mystical experience undergoes transformation of character, growing in God's traits of "love, gentleness, tenderness and self-giving grace." His ethical life blossoms; his spiritual power intensifies. He is "possessed with a new and deeper passion to have his life turned into a living radiation-centre of the Kingdom of God. . . ."[16]

Is such rich experience possible for everyone, or is it limited to the gifted, specially blessed few? Certainly history has recorded only a few truly great mystics, and Jones regarded these as religious geniuses, limited in number as are geniuses in all fields. But what of the nongenius, the everyday sort of person? Jones had difficulty making up his mind. In one book he would suggest that mystical experience is for the many; in another, that it is by no means open to everyone. In his last book he came down on the democratic side, pointing to the Quaker theory that all human beings receive the divine Light, and declaring that "the mystical trait . . . is not in any true sense confined to a small chosen list. . . ."[17]

Of all the intellectual problems with which Jones wrestled, the one that gave him at least as much if not more trouble than any other was his distinction between "affirmative mysticism" and "the so-called *via negativa* type of mystical contemplation." Basic to the negative way, as he saw it, was the classic concept of an ineffable God of whom truth could be uttered only by negatives—not this, not that. It was a concept of which he disapproved, a forbidding "theory of the abstract infinite." Instead of pointing out the "deeper yes" of the negatives, as William James had done, he suggested that the "theory of the abstract (i.e. characterless) infinite" would lead the mystic "to expect his experience of God to terminate on a mental blank, an everlasting Nay. . . ." It would also lead him to suppose that the only way to reach the divine Alone was ecstatic flight beyond all temporal reality; and ecstasy, Jones noted, sometimes "betokens abnormality." He was equally uneasy with the negative way's emphasis upon seeking the ultimate Godhead by surrendering all worldly desire and completely dying to self. Though he conceded that the mystical experience entailed this to some degree, he maintained that the great mystics had managed to live "rich concrete" lives only by "neglecting to be consistent with . . . rigorous negation and abstraction." All things considered, he held that in Christian mysticism the classic concept of the ineffable God was a most unfortunate heritage. It was not the revealed truth of mystical experience but a fallacious metaphysical interpretation of such experience. And sweepingly he declared, "The long struggle of man's mind with the stern compulsions of this abstract infinite is, I think, one of the major intellectual tragedies of human life."[18]

Far different from the deity of the negative way, he felt, was the concrete, self-revealing God of love, *agape*, in whom he believed. This God was found in "a type of mysticism quite emphatically *affirmative*," which had been "set forth in vivid style by Saint Paul and Saint John some centuries before the negative pattern of mysticism came into vogue in Europe through the writings of Dionysius." Other exponents of "the Divine Yes" were the spiritual reformers whose history he had written, men like Hans Denck, Peter Sterry, and Jacob Boehme, who created their "fresh affirmative mysticism" out of "the strand of mysticism which had come from 'the Friends of God,' the humanism of Erasmus, the inward religion of Luther's early insight and withal the glowing message of the New Testament. . . ." Still others were George Fox and his first followers. In Jones' analysis the spiritual reformers led to the Quakers, and affirmative mysticism became essentially the Quaker mysticism of his personal experience, which dispensed with elaborate theology and mystical discipline, was mild rather than ecstatic, and combined the seeking of the Inner Light with emphasis upon spiritual enrichment of the personality and active service in the world on behalf of God and man.[19]

Throughout his career Jones advocated affirmative mysticism, never wavering in his conviction that it was superior to the negative way. In 1945, Aldous Huxley published *The Perennial Philosophy*, an anthology of mysticism that made no distinction between affirmative and negative types. Two years later, in *The Luminous Trail*, Jones explicitly took issue with Huxley. He praised Huxley's interpretive power and the richness of his selections from the great mystical writings of the world, but objected that the perennial philosophy was presented solely as "a *via negativa.*" Especially did Huxley emphasize, through quotation and analysis, the perennial mystical insistence on permanently negating the self, the ego, and Jones did not like the idea of permanent self-loss. In *Social Law* he had written of the mystical experience, "To become one with God in a conscious union is the goal. To know that our being has been taken up and made an organic part of His very self, because He wills and because we will it, is the end of true mysticism. The 'I' and the 'thou' are lost only as they are always lost in love. They are lost to be found again enriched." In *The Luminous Trail* he conceded that "there is an element of truth in this insistence on the severe reduction of self-importance. *Egoism* is an undoubted hindrance, not only to the religious life, but to the social life as well, even on the purely human level." But the effort at complete self-naughting, carried seriously to its limit, "means . . . that you cease to be a person at all, and I assume that the major business we are here for in this world is to be a rightly fashioned person as an organ of the divine purpose." There was a better mystical way than the negative, he contended—the affirmative way—and he went on to pile up quotations from St. Paul and other mystical writers which illustrated his belief in a concrete self-revealing Infinite, the "Divine Yes."[20]

This was not just argument for argument's sake. Jones was defending a central position in his religious thought. Through all his writings from *Social Law* onward, he stated in 1932, he had been trying to leave the "abstract Infinite behind where it belongs and to pass over to an interpretation of God which brings 'the two worlds' together into a single unity and which finds Him actually *revealed* in the moral demonstrations of history, in the highest reaches of humanity, above all in a divine-human Person, in the validity of truth and beauty and love and goodness as we know them, and in the finite-infinite nature of our own self-consciousness as persons."[21]

By the thirties and forties his argument against the negative way had become more uncompromising than it had once been. When in 1924, in *Fundamental Ends of Life,* he wrote of affirmative and negation mysticism, he explained that "the difference between the two types is a relative difference. There have been no negation mystics who were not also affirmative, and there neither are, nor will be any important affirmation mystics who do not tread at some point the *via negativa*—the hard and dolorous road." The student of his mystical thought may feel that he needed to emphasize this relative difference more fully and more often than he later did.

But he was convinced that the negative way, though undeniably a fruitful one for great mystics of the past, was not "a *live* hypothesis" in the twentieth century. If mysticism was "to make any vital appeal" to the men of his day, "it must be interpreted in current terms of thought,"[22] and persistently he sought to refashion old ideas to meet the needs of his own time and place. The Quaker mysticism that he advocated and practiced was grounded in modern philosophy and cognizant of the latest developments in psychology and the other sciences. It emphasized, for worldly-minded, individualistic Western man, the availability of the Infinite within the finite, the spiritual enrichment of the personality, and the virtue of social service. A complex of ideas rather than a fully developed system, it did not earn Rufus Jones a permanent place of importance in the philosophy of religion. But it did earn him an international reputation as an outstanding Christian mystic, and as such his place in religious thought seems secure.

In 1936, while Rufus Jones was living in academic retirement at Haverford, a forty-three-year-old Quaker named Thomas Raymond Kelly joined the college philosophy department. Though no one knew it at the time, least of all Kelly, he was nearing the end of a painful self-naughting process that would lead to mystical experience. The invisible cross that Kelly bore was ambition, consuming ambition which seemed to stem from the insecurity that was the pattern of his life.

Born of Quaker parents on an Ohio farm, at the age of four he had seen his father die and his mother begin a long struggle for food and clothing and education for himself and his older sister. His boyhood was lonely and unhappy, and as he matured he entered upon a relentless drive for academic achievement. After graduating from Wilmington College, Ohio, in 1913 and then taking a second bachelor's degree at Haverford, where he gained the friendship of Rufus Jones, he combined teaching with graduate study. A Bachelor of Divinity degree from Hartford Theological Seminary in 1919 was followed by the Ph.D. in philosophy from Hartford in 1924 and by two years of postdoctoral study at Harvard University, 1930–32, under the direction of Professor Alfred North Whitehead. During this twenty-year period he also married and began rearing a family, performed Quaker service abroad during and after the first world war, and moved from one teaching position to another in a restless quest for intellectual satisfaction, staying longest at Earlham College, Indiana.

At Haverford the academic community could see something of his complex personality. He was the austere scholar dedicated to the rigorous search for philosophical truth, the able classroom teacher, the personable, laughing man who drew students and colleagues to him, the devout Quaker with an interest in mysticism, the eloquent minister much in demand at Quaker meetings. His wife and intimate friends knew that the years of straining after scholarly goals had burdened him with debt and impaired his health; in December, 1934, he had suffered a nervous breakdown from which it took several months to recover. And though Haverford satisfied his ambition for a permanent teaching position at a good Eastern school, he still felt intellectually unfulfilled. He wanted a Harvard degree in his field, and with some difficulty he had persuaded the Harvard Graduate School to let him work toward a second doctorate, offering as his thesis, under Whitehead, a study of the thought of the French philosopher, Emile Meyerson. In 1935 the dissertation had been accepted and approved at Harvard, and since then Kelly had been trying to get it published. He was told that because it was a technical study, of interest to a limited reading audience, he must pay a heavy subsidy to put it into print. By borrowing against his life insurance he raised the necessary money, and in the summer of 1937 the Princeton University Press published *Explanation and Reality in the Philosophy of Emile Meyerson*, a work that was received not uncritically but with respect by specialists in philosophy.

Thomas Kelly was on the brink of realizing all his ambitions. A good teaching position and scholarly publication had been attained. Now all that remained was to pass his final oral examination, and the long-sought Harvard doctorate would be his. That fall he went to Cambridge for the examination. His mind blanked and he failed, so badly that he was told he could never again try for the degree.

"It was as if the world had caved in on him," writes his son, Richard M. Kelly. "He was not the first man to have failed at Harvard, but the goal of the Ph.D. seems to have symbolized more in his mind than the degree itself. It was to have been the justification of the years of struggle and labor. It represented the crushing debts. . . . the repeated uprooting of his family. It represented his broken health. It represented his quest for perfection and self-sufficiency and scholarship which had led him so far from the religious consecration of his youth."[23]

So intense was his despair that his wife feared he might commit suicide or lapse into permanent mental depression. His friend Douglas V. Steere, who was head of the Haverford philosophy department, came to his home and talked with him for hours, assuring him that his position at Haverford was secure. The college president also visited him to affirm this and to assure him that the failure could be kept secret. Their kind words were not enough. Thomas Kelly was suffering the crucifixion of self.

Then, during the ensuing winter, came mystical experience. Kelly described it as being "much shaken by the experience of Presence—something that I did not seek, but that *sought* me." His character changed. "He moved toward adequacy," says Steere. "A fissure in him seemed to close . . . what was divided grew together within him. Science, scholarship, method, remained good, but in a new setting." When in January 1938 he gave three lectures at the Germantown Friends' Meeting, "people were deeply moved and said, 'This is *authentic.*'" The following April he wrote Rufus Jones, "The reality of Presence has been very great at times recently."[24]

That summer he went abroad. As a representative of the American Friends Service Committee, he spent three months in Germany, traveling from one city to another, living in the homes of Quakers, meditating with them, and discussing with them the problems of daily life under the Hitler dictatorship. He was shocked by what he learned of the raw brutality of Nazism and the suffering of its victims, yet inspired by the courage and religious devotion of the people he met, and by the warm fellowship they extended to him. During his stay he encountered a number of men and women who were on the mystical pathway that he also had found, and with them he had deeply moving experiences of the Presence. These special persons belonged to no particular class or nationality. "One Frenchman is one of the most profound mystics I have met," Kelly wrote his wife from Nürnberg on August 31. "The amazing life of inner spirit which he has makes me leap for joy. For something of the same sort has been happening to me, and I have been just plowed down to depths I've never known before."[25]

When he returned to the United States in September, he told Douglas Steere, "It is wonderful. I have been literally melted down by the love of God." And in a letter of September 26 to Rufus Jones he wrote, "I have had this summer, and still have, such a sweeping experience of 'refreshment of the spirit' so amazing, so sweet, and so prolonged as to go clear down to the roots of my being."[26]

His mystical experiences continued intermittently until January 1941. Then, without warning, came death. On the morning of January 17 while conversing with his wife he exclaimed, "Today will be the greatest day of my life!" That evening, as his son describes it, "he suffered a massive heart attack and was dead within moments."[27]

In the years that followed, his ideas reached a much wider audience than he had known in life. His mystical lectures and essays, a number of which had previously been published in the Philadelphia journal, *The Friend*, were brought together in book form. A little volume of five of these writings, with a biographical memoir by Douglas Steere, came out in 1941 under the title, *A Testament of Devotion*. It has become an enduring classic of modern mysticism. Four other lectures were printed in 1942 as a pamphlet, *Reality of the Spiritual World*. In 1966 Richard M. Kelly published *Thomas Kelly: A Biography*, in which he quotes at length from letters by his father, and *The Eternal Promise*, an edition of Thomas Kelly articles compiled from various periodicals.

In all these writings Thomas Kelly reports and interprets his mystical experience by means of Quaker concepts similar to those of Rufus Jones. To a lesser degree than Jones he also draws upon other mystical writers, naming as his "three dearest spiritual friends and patterns, outside of Jesus of Nazareth," St. Francis of Assisi, John Woolman, and Brother Lawrence, the seventeenth-century lay brother of the Carmelite Order who was noted for his practice of the presence of God.[28] The simple piety that characterizes these three spiritual models is the keynote of Kelly's mysticism.

Indeed it is more than the keynote. It is the overwhelmingly dominant element which all but excludes from his mystical writings the learned scholar who had entered theology and philosophy through natural science, who had written his doctoral dissertation at Hartford on "The Place of Value Judgments in the Philosophy of Hermann Lotze," who had drunk deeply and enthusiastically of Whitehead's realism and published a critical study of Emile Meyerson's epistemology; who had an abiding interest in Oriental thought and at Haverford studied Sanskrit and Chinese while teaching a survey of Indian philosophy. In 1934, at a time when any mystical feeling that he may have had was submerged in intellectuality, Kelly could include in a rationalistic lecture on philosophy, natural science, and religion as "three major fields in the Quest for Reality" the circumpsect statement that "mystics claim to have touched reality and been in contact with it." A few years later, after he had been "shaken by the experience of Presence," he could say to another audience, "To you in this room who are seekers . . . I want to speak as simply, as tenderly, as clearly as I can. For God *can* be found . . . . There is a Divine Center into which your life can slip, a new and absolute orientation in God, a Center where you live with Him and out of which you see all of life, through new and radiant vision, tinged with new sorrows and pangs, new joys unspeakable and full of glory."[29]

In the last sentence of this statement the word "new" is used four times. Here Kelly is not the philosopher analyzing but the "new man" testifying. And so it is throughout his mystical writings. Again and again he bypasses the philosophical approach and simply describes his own experience. "There come times when the Presence *steals upon us*, all unexpected not the product of agonized effort, and we live in a new dimension of life," he said on one occasion. "You who have experienced such plateaus of glory know what I mean. . . . One walks in the world yet above the world as well, giddy with the height, with feather tread, with effortlessness and calm security, meeting the daily routine, yet never losing the sense of Presence. Sometimes these periods are acute and brief, too dazzling to report to anyone. Sometimes they are less elevated but more prolonged, with a milder sense of glory and of lift, yet as surely of a piece with the more acute experience." He went on to tell how Rufus Jones' friend John Wilhelm Rowntree had suddenly been enfolded with the love and joy of God just after his physician had warned him that his failing eyesight would end in blindness. "I cannot report such a timeliness of visitation," he then added, "but only unpredictable arrivals and fadings-out."

When he discussed the immediate fruits of such visitation he said, "Then is the soul swept into a Loving Center of ineffable sweetness, where calm and unspeakable peace and ravishing joy steal over one. And one knows now why Pascal wrote, in the center of his greatest moment, the single word, 'Fire.' " On the sense of joy he elaborated, "And one sings inexpressibly sweet songs within oneself, and one *tries* to keep one's inner hilarity and exuberance within bonds lest, like the men of Pentecost, we be mistaken for men filled with new wine. Traditional Quaker decorum and this burning experience of a Living Presence are only with the greatest difficulty held together!" In the Loving Center, he further reported, the fruit was received with astonishment. "One may have said all one's life, *God is Love*. But there is an experience of the love of God which, when it comes upon us, and enfolds us, and bathes us, and warms us, is so utterly new that we can hardly identify it with the old phrase, God is love. Can *this* be the love of God, this burning, tender, wooing, wounding pain of love that pierces the marrow of my bones and burns out old loves and ambitions? God experienced is a vast surprise."

Was such frank testimony immodest? Kelly was aware that some might so regard it. That there was "an indelicacy in too-ready speech" he admitted. "But there is also a false reticence," he argued, "as if these things were one's own work and one's own possession, about which we should modestly keep quiet, whereas they are wholly God's amazing work and we are nothing, mere passive receivers."[30]

From all that he said and wrote, it seems evident that his most intense mystical experiences came to him in solitude. But he also speaks of experiencing Presence in company with one or two friends and in Quaker "covered" or "gathered" meetings, which he describes as follows: "In the practice of group worship on the basis of silence come special times when the electric hush and solemnity and depth of power steals over the worshipers. A blanket of divine covering comes over the room. . . . A quickening Presence pervades us, breaking down some part of the special privacy and isolation of our individual Life and Power. . . . Such gathered meetings I take to be cases of group mysticism." Comparatively mild mysticism, to be sure, "yet really of a piece with all mystical experience. For mystical times are capable of all gradings and shadings, from sublime heights to very mild moments of lift and very faint glimpses of glory."

From this description of the gathered meeting Kelly passes to analysis of it, and his interest in science and philosophy emerges. As group mysticism, he suggests, the gathered meeting shows William James' marks of ineffability, noetic quality, transiency, and passivity. The sense of passivity persists even when the silence is broken, in accordance with Quaker custom, by spontaneous speech; for "when one rises to speak in such a meeting," one has "a sense of *being used,* of being played upon, of being spoken through. It is as amazing an experience as that of being *prayed through,* when we, the praying ones, are no longer the initiators of the supplication, but seem to be transmitters. . . ." Further he suggests "a fifth trait of mystical experience" that might "well be added to James' list." This is "the sense of unity, unity with the Divine Life who has graciously allowed us to

43

touch the hem of His garment, unity with our fellow worshipers, for He has broken down the middle wall of partition between our separate personalities and has flooded us with a sense of *fellowship.*"

In short, Kelly is convinced that the gathered meeting is grounded in "the Real Presence of God." Rejecting the notion that the "sense of covering" can be dismissed as "a mere psychological phenomenon," he argues that in the same way the psychological tag can be applied to *"all* that we think and experience"—beauty, political ideas, historical events, even the natural sciences and mathematics. To apply the term so broadly is to indulge in what the Germans call *Psychologismus.* "And on this platform of *Psychologismus* all of religious experience becomes 'merely psychological,' and, presumably, merely subjective. Not only would mysticism lose its claim to be substantially real, resting not upon subjective changes in the human person, but upon the real activity of an existent, self-revealing God, but also prayer, praise, thanksgiving, sin, forgiveness would all become 'merely psychological,' merely subjective." Kelly therefore rejects *Psychologismus* and aligns himself with twentieth-century realism, which he views as "opening the gates again to the contention of the mystics, that mystical experience is not merely a matter of subjective states but a matter of objective reality."[31]

Though he believes in the validity of mystical experience, whether that of the individual or of the gathered meeting, he holds that in the final analysis this belief must rest not upon logical proof but upon faith. For example, the mystic often feels intensely certain that he has found God, but "mere internal pressure of certainty does not prove certainty. . . . The insane hospitals are full of people who have intense internal certainties that they are Jesus Christ, or Napoleon, or an angel from heaven." Even the evidence of the transformed life, which "not only Rufus Jones but all other writers on the subject" employ, is not flawless to the mind of the logician; for when the argument from the evidence of the transformed life is examined in syllogistic form it is found to contain the logical fallacy of affirming the consequent. However, experimental science rests upon the same fallacy—therefore "upon faith, not upon certainty"—and like the scientist the religious seeker need not be disturbed. "I am persuaded that God is greater than logic, although not contrary to logic," affirms Kelly, "and our mere inability to catch Him in the little net of our human reason is no proof of His non-existence, but only of our need that our little reason shall be supplemented by His tender visitations, and that He may lead and guide us to the end of the road in ways superior to any that our intellects can plan."[32]

However desirable mystical experience might be, and plainly Kelly places it among the greatest blessings, he does not regard it as essential to the good religious life. "It would be a tragic mistake," he declares, "to suppose that religion is only for a small group, who have certain vivid but transient inner experiences. . . ." What is essential to genuine religious dedication is will, not clench-jawed "I will" but humble, persistent effort to practice "holy obedience," to engage in "glad willing away of self," and lose one's own will in the will of God.[33]

On the question of selflessness Kelly differs implicitly from Rufus Jones. Explicitly he writes, much like Jones, that "according to our Christian conception of the unselfing in religion, to become unselfed is to become truly integrated as a richer self." But this is the theme of only one paragraph in one lecture. In contrast, Kelly repeatedly connects selflessness and mystical experience without mentioning a resultant integrated personality. Writing to his wife from Germany in 1938 he remarks how his experience of Presence "takes away the old self-seeking, self-centered self, from which selfishness I have laid heavy burdens on you, dear one. Help me, sweetheart, to become more like a little child—not proud of learning, not ambitious for self, but emptied of these things, and guided by that amazing Power, which is so gentle." In his lecture "Holy Obedience" he tells how the Presence "leaves one's old proud self utterly, utterly defenseless," but warns that afterward there is subtle danger; for "O how slick and weasel-like is self-pride!" The seeker who escapes the danger finds that one of the fruits of his holy obedience is "the sense of utter humility." For God, "in His glorious otherness, empties us of ourselves in order that He may become all."[34] Thus Kelly speaks of selflessness not as merely the avoidance of egoism but as self-naughting. It is one of his major themes.

Another is suffering. The suffering both physical and mental that he saw so many enduring in Hitler's Germany burned deep into his mind; he suffered vicariously with the victims of Nazism. "He told several of his student friends later," writes Douglas Steere, "of a specific experience that he had had on his knees in the great cathedral at Cologne where he seemed to feel God laying the whole congealed suffering of humanity upon his heart —a burden too terrible to be borne—but yet with His help bearable."[35]

What did it mean, this anguish of mankind that he felt so keenly and saw all around him in Germany? How should one regard it, how reconcile it with one's faith in the Christian God of love? In his lecture-essays Kelly does not, like a Josiah Royce, attempt final philosophical answers to the problem of Job, but comments upon it as a mystic.

He feels that compared to the tortured lives he has seen his own "has not been hard," and that he speaks not as one who has himself suffered but as a witness made newly sensitive through mystical experience, "the dawning experience of the living Christ" who as Jesus of Nazareth endured the Cross. The "God-blinded soul" has "excruciatingly sensitive eyesight toward the world of men," and is confronted with the religious paradox: " 'Nothing matters; everything matters.' " And he knows, like the Hindu monk with whom, Kelly says, he discussed the paradox, that while some suffering can be removed "there is an inexorable residue which confronts you and me and the blighted souls of Europe and China and the Near East and India. . . ." This inexorable experience is not inevitably purifying; suffering does not automatically "shake great souls into life"; to the contrary, it can "blast and blight an earnest but unprepared soul, and

46

damn it utterly to despair." Hope lies in preparedness. Those who enter suffering prepared through awareness of the Inner Light, the "seed of Christ" within them, can willingly receive their Cross. For, "where this seed of divine awareness is quickened and grows, there Calvary is enacted again in joy. And Calvary is still the hope of the world."

And here in Kelly's thought, it seems, suffering merges with selflessness. His solution to the problem of evil appears to be the mystical self-naughting which joyfully surrenders to God all worldly desire, even the desire to escape suffering. Beneath this ultimate concept he crushes the philosophy of the Declaration of Independence. "Our right to life, liberty, and the pursuit of happiness is not absolute. We dare not claim them as our absolute right. For the seed of Christ that we bear into the world's suffering will teach us to *renounce* these as our own, and strip us, in utter poverty of soul and perhaps of body, until our only hope is in the eternal goodness of God."[36]

The passivity of this thoroughgoing mysticism does not make Kelly indifferent to all efforts to alleviate the sorrows of the world. He is too much the active Quaker to embrace quietism. He advocates social service in Quaker work camps, and stresses the desirability of "having a concern" to perform a special task for the benefit of others. But to his mind much of the virtue of the Quaker "concern" lies in its limiting function. It not only particularizes "the Divine Concern of God for all creation," but also particularizes *"my* responsibility . . . in a world too vast and a lifetime too short for me to carry all responsibilities." One should be sympathetic toward all the good tasks that need doing, but select only a few as one's special concerns. Kelly deplores both the heroic-minded religious activist who like a Nietzchean superman attempts to attack and demolish all the world's problems and his success-minded colleague who constantly strains to "work hard and please God and make a good record and bring in the kingdom!" The mystic knows that God does not need such fevered service. Nor does he accept the modern belief that the worth of Eternity must be measured by "the benefits it may

47

possibly bring to affairs in time." Certainly Kelly does not accept it. "Time is no judge of Eternity," he declares. "It is the Eternal who is the judge and tester of time"[37]

To Kelly the mystic the Eternal is intimately real. Like an American Brother Lawrence he writes of the joy of practicing the presence of God, and tells how he has gradually developed the ability to live simultaneously in the world of his daily tasks and in the Eternal Now. His method, he explains, is Brother Lawrence's—the simple art of continually turning one's mind to God in prayer and adoration. Though simple this is not easy, yet Kelly believes that all who humbly and sincerely persist in the art will acquire facility in it. And repeatedly in his lectures he urges his listeners to begin immediately the joyous practice of dwelling continually in the divine Center.[38]

Closely related to this life in the Center is one of Kelly's most vivid concepts—that of "the Blessed Community." One discovers the Community, he affirms, through mystical experience. "When our souls are utterly swept through and overturned by God's invading love, we suddenly find ourselves in the midst of a wholly new relationship with some of our fellow-men." Through eyes from which the scales have fallen we see that certain persons whose religious life we formerly admired have relatively little spiritual depth, while others who in their humility had gone unnoticed by us stand revealed as saints dwelling "down in the center in Christ." These saints are our true friends, we realize, and we begin a mystical association with them so profound that the word "fellowship" only faintly describes it. Through God's grace we have entered "the Blessed Community." Within it, one finds no barriers. There are no barriers of time: one lives with the great mystics of the past in new appreciation of their writings. There are no barriers of place: Thomas Kelly in America feels the "amazing bondedness of divine love" uniting him with the mystics he has met in Europe. There are no barriers of class: a professor may learn spiritual lessons from a day laborer, as Kelly was taught by a stooped, ungrammatical factory worker when he visited the man's home near Stuttgart and found himself in immediate rapport with "a quiet, reticent saint of God." There are no barriers of nationality, race, or religious creed. The members of the Community do not measure man by such notions. They dwell harmoniously together in mystical unity with God, "upholding one another by internal bonds of prayer," and extending to each person they meet that "Eternal Love" which Kelly would like to see illuminating all human relations. "For until the life of men in time is, in every relation, shot through with Eternity," he writes, "the Blessed Community is not complete."[39]

Eternity! This surely is the realm in which Kelly the mystical thinker almost continually dwells, in contrast to Rufus Jones, who can and does write eloquently of Eternity but also deals at length with more worldly subjects like history and philosophy. Had Kelly lived to elaborate his thought as extensively as Jones did his, doubtless the marked personal quality of it would have been somewhat diffused. Yet one feels that personal testimony would still be its keynote. Kelly seems to be the kind of mystic who must perforce embed his ideas in commentary upon his own mystical experience. Unlike Jones he is not concerned with modernizing old concepts, with drawing distinctions between affirmative and negative mysticism, or with combating the idea of self-naughting, which indeed he seems to accept. Rather he delights in describing how he experienced states of mystical consciousness that seem to have verged, at times, into ecstasy. His reiterated message—one might almost call it song—is Joy! I have found Him! You can find Him, too. Coupled with it is deep awareness of suffering, which yet does not efface joy in the triumph of Calvary. In all this Kelly seems closer to traditional European mysticism than to the modern outlook of Rufus Jones.

In breadth and depth of scholarship and in fullness of thought Kelly's scattering of mystical essays is of course greatly outweighed by Jones' many books. But one thing Kelly seems to have in richer abundance than his more famous contemporary: mystical experience; and untiringly he describes it in prose that is sometimes rough-hewn, sometimes boyishly naïve, but invariably intense. If Jones' thought is the impressive, mellow glow of mysticism, Kelly's is the flame. For nearly three decades it has been burning in its niche in the American pantheon, and it shows no sign of going out.

CHAPTER 4

Three Varieties of Mysticism

In America as elsewhere the Judaeo-Christian tradition has encompassed many mansions of the mind and spirit. Within it have flourished not only the Quaker way of Rufus Jones and Thomas Kelly but also other varieties of mysticism. Let us now consider three of these varieties, as exemplified in the lives and thought of three gifted men—Howard Thurman, Abraham Joshua Heschel, and Thomas Merton.

Although as a mystic Thurman has much in common with Rufus Jones, who helped to mold his thinking, he is notably different from the Quaker theologian because of one salient factor. His skin is black. He knows color barriers in America in a way no white man can ever know them.

Today Thurman is an elder statesman of American religion, and on the surface his record of achievement gives little indication of barriers, or of the cruel blows that racial discrimination deals against human dignity. Co-founder and pastor of the Church for the Fellowship of All Peoples, in San Francisco, Dean of Marsh Chapel and Professor of Spiritual Disciplines and Resources at Boston University, guest lecturer at Harvard and other leading universities, author of fifteen books—all this bespeaks triumph, not frustration. But the surface record does not, of course, reveal the whole man. When in 1961 Thurman gave the Rufus Jones Lecture at Baltimore Friends School, he spoke on

"Mysticism and the Experience of Love," and explained at the outset that the inner life is his fortress against racial discrimination.

He believes, he said, that

a man can seek deliberately to explore the inner region and resources of his own life. . . . He can become at home *within* by locating in his own spirit the trysting place where he and God may meet. . . . For me the choice is personal because all my life I have been seeking to validate, beyond all ambivalences and frustrations, the integrity of the inner life. I have sensed the urgency to find a way to act and react responsibly out of my own center. I have sought a way of life that could come under the influence of, and be informed by, the fruits of the inner life. The cruel vicissitudes of the social situation in which I have been forced to live in American society have made it vital for me to seek resources, or a resource, to which I could have access as I sought means for sustaining the personal enterprise of my life beyond all of the ravages inflicted upon it by the brutalities of the social order. To live under siege, with the equilibrium and tranquillity of peace, to prevent the springs of my being from being polluted by the bitter fruit of the climate of violence, to hold and re-hold the moral initiative of my own action and to seek the experience of community, all of this to whatever extent it has been possible to achieve it, is to walk through a door that no man can shut.[1]

That in contrast men can and do shut worldly doors Howard Thurman well knows. The lesson thrust itself unforgettably upon him during his boyhood in Daytona Beach, Florida, where he was born in 1900. As a black boy he had to have a letter of authorization signed by a white man before he could cross the river at night from the Negro to the white section of the town. His schooling was supposed to stop with the seventh grade. Only the kindness of his principal, who tutored him at the noon recess, enabled him to obtain the eighth-grade diploma that made higher education possible. Even men of his own race, he found, could occasionally shut doors. The deacons of the Baptist church in his community were not impressed by his religious thoughts and feelings and declined to baptize him until his grandmother marched him before the board and demanded, "How dare you men stand between this boy and God?"[2]

His grandmother and his mother, a widow who supported her family by doing housework in the white part of town, reared him in the Protestant ethic of strict discipline, honesty, piety, and material progress through thrift and hard work. They also taught him to avoid conflict with the dominant white people, and in this he was largely successful. But he could not escape the knowledge that they considered him an inferior species. When he least expected it, some little incident would occur to remind him of this prejudice.

But there was comfort and hope in religion, and hope also in education, and on these foundations Howard Thurman built his career. Aided by relatives and friends, he worked his way through high school, college, and graduate studies, receiving his high-school certificate from Florida Baptist Academy; his Bachelor of Arts degree from Morehouse College, in 1923; his ordination as a Baptist minister in 1925; and his Bachelor of Divinity degree from Rochester Theological Seminary in 1926. In the same year he married, and became pastor of Mt. Zion Baptist Church in Oberlin, Ohio. Then in 1928 he was appointed professor of religion at Morehouse. The path of teaching, merging with that of ministerial service, would lead onward to Howard and Boston universities.

While at Oberlin, Thurman read one of Rufus Jones' books, felt instant rapport with the Quaker mystic's religious thought, got in touch with him through a mutual friend, and wrote him that he would like to study privately under his guidance, adding, "My color is black." Jones replied, without mentioning color, that he could make arrangements for Thurman to live in Graduate House at Haverford and audit his courses, including the weekly seminar that he taught on Meister Eckhart. About this time Thurman received his appointment to Morehouse, and also a Charles Fisher Kent Fellowship granted by the National Council on Religion in Higher Education.

But tragedy overshadowed good fortune. Thurman's wife Katie was in poor health, and shortly after he moved with her and their small daughter to Atlanta, Georgia, to begin his work at

Morehouse, she died. The meaning of sorrow came home to Thurman in its starkest terms. It was intimately personal, now. It dwelt with him.

He obtained a year's leave of absence from Morehouse, sent his daughter to stay with her grandmother, and went to Haverford in January 1930 to study with Rufus Jones. It was the great turning point of his life. Jones taught him the meaning of mysticism, and immersed him in its literature and in the Quaker method of meditation.[3]

Mystical experience was not new to him. It had been a part of his life since boyhood, as this autobiographical passage from one of his books reveals:

As a child I was accustomed to spend many hours alone in my rowboat, fishing along the river, when there was no sound save the lapping of the waves against the boat. There were times when it seemed as if the earth and the river and the sky and I were one beat of the same pulse. It was a time of watching and waiting for what I did not know—yet I always knew. There would come a moment when beyond the single pulse beat there was a sense of Presence which seemed always to speak to me. My response to the sense of Presence always had the quality of personal communion. There was no voice. There was no image. There was no vision. There was God.[4]

But if mystical experience was not new, the interpretation of it—the mysticism—that Jones taught opened fresh worlds before him. "It was far more exciting than I have words to express," he said afterward, "to discover that what I had sensed and experienced in my own spiritual journey was a part of the movement of the spirit of God in the life of men through the ages." He and his teacher engaged in enthusiastic discussions of God and the Inner Light. "But it almost seems sacrilege to pray to Him!" Thurman exclaimed on one occasion, and ever afterward cherished Jones' reply that "the soul of a man should enjoy God," and pray to Him "out of sheer love."[5]

At Haverford, then, Thurman gained the religious strength of mysticism, and in 1932 he gained the companionship of a second wife, Sue Bailey, who bore him another daughter. Years of teaching and preaching followed. In 1945 he published the first of his books, and thereafter they multiplied rapidly.

They are not weighty theological treatises, but relatively brief inspirational works; collections of sermons and of meditations in prose and poetry, autobiographical narrative, and commentary on various religious and social subjects, including racial discrimination in America. Here and there one finds further revelation of Thurman's personal mystical experience. For example:

> Each soul must learn to stand up in its own right and live. How blissful to lean upon another, to seek a sense of everlasting arms expressed in the vitality of a friend! We walk a part of the way together, but on the upper reaches of life, each path takes its way to the heights —alone. Ultimately, I am alone, so vastly alone that in my aloneness is all the life of the universe. Stripped to the literal substance of myself, there is nothing left but naked soul, the irreducible ground of individual being, which becomes at once the quickening throb of God. At such moments of profound awareness I seem to be all that there is in the world, and all that there is in the world seems to be myself.[6]

And again, this meditative prayer:

> In Thy Presence we become aware of many divisions within the inner circle of the Self. When we enter into communion with Thee, we are never sure of the Voice that speaks within us. We do not always know which voice is the true Voice. . . . In the midst of all the sounds rising above all the mingled words there is a strange Voice—but not quite a stranger. A man recognizes it. It seems to come from every part of him but cannot rest itself on any point of sound. He waits. He listens. When all is still, he listens now at a deeper level of silence. In soundless movement there floats up through all the chambers of his being, encompassing all the tongued cries from many selves, one word: God—God —God. And the answer is the same, filling all the living silence before Thy Face: God—God—God.[7]

Thurman's mysticism is not Quaker. He does not stress the Inner Light concept of the Friends. But he acknowledges the influence of Rufus Jones on his religious thought. He accepts Jones' definition of mysticism, and defines it himself as "the response of the individual to a personal encounter with God within his own spirit." It was Jones, he says, who gave him confidence that "the religion of the inner life at its best is life affirming rather than life denying and must forever be involved in the Master's instruction, 'Be ye perfect, even as your heavenly father is perfect.' "[8]

The phrase "life affirming rather than life denying" seems to endorse Jones' argument against the *via negativa;* however, that debate is not one of Thurman's main concerns. Indeed, in his writings he repeatedly emphasizes, without qualification, the importance of selflessness. "The central element in communion with God," he states, "is the act of self-surrender." Yet, like Jones, he holds that "in the surrender to God in the religious experience there is no loss of being"; rather, the surrendered person "literally . . . loses his life and finds it" again at a higher level of moral effort.[9]

When Thurman speaks of "life affirming," he seems also to have in mind his mystical faith that since life flows from God it is good, and "will not ultimately sustain evil." High on the list of evils over which he expects good ultimately to triumph is racial injustice. In keeping with his view that "we must not shrink from the knowledge of the evilness of evil,"[10] he has written two books dealing with the challenge that racial injustice in the United States poses to Christianity. The challenge was put to him, as a Christian, in Ceylon in the fall of 1935, while he was serving as chairman of a friendship delegation from the students of America to the students of India, Burma, and Ceylon. After he had spoken before the Law College of the University of Colombo on civil disabilities under states' rights in America, the principal of the college, who was a Hindu, entertained him at coffee and bluntly asked him why he, a Negro, was in Ceylon advocating Christianity. His African forefathers had been enslaved by Christians, the principal reminded him; and though slavery in America had been abolished, he and his fellow Negroes lived "in a Christian nation in which you are segregated, lynched, and burned."[11]

Out of the five-hour discussion that followed this indictment, Thurman developed his book *Jesus and the Disinherited* (1949), in which he suggests that under the rule of Rome the Jews of Palestine in Jesus' day were an oppressed minority like the Negroes of modern America, and asks what Jesus teaches the oppressed. He teaches, says Thurman, humility, fearlessness, utter sincerity, and love—love even of one's enemies. Love overcomes hate, which destroys men's souls; and hatred, it should be remembered, is a virus to which the oppressed is no less susceptible than the oppressor.

Love of your enemy is most easily achieved, Thurman further suggests, when his enemy status can be changed so that you can associate with him on a basis of genuine fellowship. Since racial segregation erects a wall against such fellowship, it is "a complete ethical and moral evil. Whatever it may do for those who dwell on either side of the wall, one thing is certain: it poisons all normal contacts of those persons involved. The first step toward love is a common sharing of a sense of mutual worth and value."[12] (These are words to inspire anyone who would oppose Christian love to racial segregation. Martin Luther King, Jr. read *Jesus and the Disinherited* while leading the successful protest movement of 1955–56 against the segregated city bus service of Montgomery, Alabama.[13])

Tragically, declares Thurman, American Christianity has "betrayed the religion of Jesus" by practicing the evil of segregation.

Churches have been established for the under-privileged, for the weak, for the poor, on the theory that they prefer to be among themselves. Churches have been established for the Chinese, the Japanese, the Korean, the Mexican, the Filipino, the Italian, and the Negro, with the same theory in mind. The result is that in the one place in which normal, free contacts might be most naturally established—in which the relations of the individual to his God should take priority over conditions of class, race, power, status, wealth, or the like—this place is one of the chief instruments for guaranteeing barriers.[14]

At the time he wrote this, Thurman was actively practicing the religion he advocated. The Church for the Fellowship of All Peoples, of which he was pastor from 1944 to 1953, eschewed segregative barriers.[15] Its brief statement of principles made this clear and, in the opening stentence, struck a quietly mystical note: "I affirm my need for a growing understanding of all men as sons of God, and I seek after a vital experience of God as revealed in Jesus of Nazareth and other great religious spirits whose fellowship with God was the foundation of their fellowship with man." The same note sounded from the pulpit when Thurman spoke.

We believe that in the presence of God with His dream of order there is neither male nor female, white nor black, Gentile nor Jew, Protestant nor Catholic, Hindu, Buddhist, nor Moslem, but a human spirit stripped to the literal substance of itself. Wherever man has the scent of the eternal unity in his spirit, he hunts for it in his home, in his work, among his friends, in his pleasures and in all the levels of his function. It is my simple faith that this is the kind of universe that sustains that kind of adventure. And what we are fumbling towards now . . . tomorrow will be the way of life for everybody![16]

Thurman taught the members of his church to meditate, and later he taught meditation to his students at Boston University. It was an art that he had begun to acquire during his seminary days, had developed in the Quaker manner under the guidance of Rufus Jones, and had learned to appreciate anew in India, where he met Rabindranath Tagore and Mahatma Gandhi, personifications of the ancient Indian tradition of daily spiritual seeking by withdrawal into inner silence.[17]

In 1963, following his retirement from Boston University, he again went abroad, on a world tour which included Africa. At the close of a lecture before the Nigerian Press Club in Ibadan, he was asked, "What is your personal reaction to the separatist movement in your country which is in fact the acceptance of segregation?" He replied that "there is a real danger inherent in accepting segregation: it could very easily cause people to feel that they are *aliens* in their own country. Once an American feels that America is not his homeland, he has given up his right to claim the fruits of citizenship."[18]

This was opposition to segregation on political grounds, which doubtless the journalists of a new nation could readily appreciate. In 1965, when Thurman published his second book on racial prejudice in America, *The Luminous Darkness*, he again considered the segregation question within the religious context, and reached conclusions similar to those he had advanced in *Jesus and the Disinherited*. "It is clear that for the Negro," he wrote, "the fundamental issue involved in the experience of segregation is the attack that it makes on his dignity and integrity."[19] He deplored the fact that "the commitment to love as it stands at the center of the Christian doctrine of God has not prevented the Christian from excluding Negroes from his Christian fellowship, nor has it prevented the Christian who is Negro from excluding white people from his Christian fellowship." To be sure, it seemed evident in 1965 that hopeful change was taking place; in the white churches, the barriers against the black man were beginning to fall. But Thurman was inclined to think that "this is the response of the church to the pressure of the secular community upon it, rather than the response of the church to the genius of the Gospel which it proclaims."

"But why has the church been such a tragic witness to its own Gospel?" he asks. "It does seem to me at times that it is because the church is not sufficiently religious. By this I mean that it is not wide open to the spirit of the living God."[20] In other words, it is not mystical enough—a criticism that many a mystic, through the ages, has leveled against the church, not necessarily with the intent to reject it completely but rather with the desire for reform.

As yet, Thurman has not produced a work devoted exclusively to mysticism. But clearly mysticism is the foundation of his thought, and the depth and feeling that it gives to his books may be the main reason why so many of them remain in print year after year. As a mystic, he can look squarely at the seamy reality of the racial prejudice that has shadowed all his days and simultaneously transcend it. He can write:

The fact that the first twenty-three years of my life were spent in Florida and in Georgia has left its scars deep in my spirit and has rendered me terribly sensitive to the churning abyss separating white

59

from black. Living outside of the region, I am aware of the national span of racial prejudice and the virus of segregation that undermines the vitality of American life. Nevertheless, a strange necessity has been laid upon me to devote my life to the central concern that transcends the walls that divide and would achieve in literal fact what is experienced as literal truth: human life is one and all men are members one of another. And this insight is spiritual and it is the hard core of religious experience.[21]

Markedly different from the religious thought of Thurman is that of Abraham Heschel, of whom one American critic has remarked, "Heschel . . . has become for many the leading Jewish theologian in this country."[22] Mysticism has been a part of Heschel's religious milieu since his boyhood. A descendant of the masters of modern Hasidism, the Jewish mystical movement which originated in eighteenth-century Poland, he was born in Warsaw in 1907 and grew up amid Hasidic influences in that city's Orthodox ghetto. He received graduate training and his doctorate in philosophy from the University of Berlin, and then began in Germany a teaching career that was interrupted in 1938 when the Nazis expelled him to Poland. Six weeks before the start of the second world war he went to England, and in 1940 he came to the United States to join the faculty of the Hebrew Union College in Cincinnati. Since 1945 he has taught at the Jewish Theological Seminary of America, where he is professor of Jewish ethics and mysticism.

While still in his teens Heschel began a prolific writing career by producing a book of Yiddish poems. Among the numerous volumes that he has since published in several languages these two major works, written in English since his arrival in America, are of special interst to the student of mysticism: *Man Is Not Alone: A Philosophy of Religion* (1951), and *God in Search of Man: A Philosophy of Judaism* (1955). He has also written "The Mystical Element in Judaism,"[23] an essay dealing with the cabala, and through many another of his works has scattered observations that have a mystical ring.

It should be noted, however, that Heschel neither calls himself a mystic nor presents his religious thought as mysticism, and that scholars who have commented on his philosophy as a whole disagree as to whether he is mystic or rationalist,[24] proving once more that it is difficult indeed to make neat file-drawer classifications of the human mind. Certainly it would be a distortion of his philosophy to label it wholly mystical. One of its main sources, for instance, is Hebrew prophecy, and in *The Prophets* (1962) Heschel argues convincingly that the encounters with God recorded of such men as Moses and Isaiah are unlike mystical experience. Still I would suggest that there are other aspects of his thought which do seem very much like mysticism. At least, they fit easily into the mystical pattern.

There are passages in his books which seem to be drawn out of his personal mystical experience. It is true that these are never couched in the first person singular (Gershom G. Scholem has pointed out that Jewish mysticism is notably lacking in mystical autobiography, in part, perhaps, because Jewish mystics have traditionally been reluctant to claim in writing that they have bridged the gulf that appears to separate man from the awesome God of Israel.[25]) It is also true that most of the passages are relatively brief hints, such as the statement, "We cannot be in rapport with the reality of the divine except for rare, fugitive moments."[26] But occasionally the mystical note rises to sustained eloquence, as though intense feeling had overcome reticence. This is from *God in Search of Man:*

Man's walled mind has no access to a ladder upon which he can, on his own strength, rise to knowledge of God. Yet his soul is endowed with translucent windows that open to the beyond. And if he rises to reach out to Him, it is a reflection of the divine light in him that gives him the power for such yearning. We are at times ablaze against and beyond our own power. . . .

For God is not always silent, and man is not always blind. His glory fills the world; His spirit hovers above the waters. There are moments in which, to use a Talmudic phrase, heaven and earth kiss each other; in which there is a lifting of the veil at the horizon of the known, opening a vision of what is eternal in time. Some of us have at least once experienced the momentous realness of God. Some of us have at least caught a glimpse of the beauty, peace, and power that flow through the souls of those who are devoted to Him.[27]

And this is found in *Man Is Not Alone*. Heschel begins with the comment that in our technological, materialistic age our world is "a vast cage within a maze," and that life within the cage drives some of us to despair.

But, then, a moment comes like a thunderbolt, in which a flash of the undisclosed rends our dark apathy asunder. It is full of overpowering brilliance, like a point in which all moments of life are focused or a thought which outweighs all thoughts ever conceived of. There is so much light in our cage, in our world, it is as if it were suspended amidst the stars. Apathy turns to splendor unawares. The ineffable has shuddered itself into the soul. . . . We are penetrated by His insight. We cannot think any more as if He were there and we here. He is both there and here. He is not *a being*, but *being in and beyond all beings*.

A tremor seizes our limbs; our nerves are struck, quiver like strings; our whole being bursts into shudders. But then a cry, wrested from our very core, fills the world around us, as if a mountain were suddenly about to place itself in front of us. It is one word: GOD. Not an emotion, a stir within us, but a power, a marvel beyond us, tearing the world apart. The word that means more than universe, more than eternity, holy, holy, holy; we cannot comprehend it. We only know it means infinitely more than we are able to echo.[28]

No wonder Reinhold Niebuhr reviewed the books containing these passages as the work of a mystic. These outbursts of prose poetry speak for themselves, and for anyone sensitive to the testimony of mystics they ring familiar bells. They help us to understand why one of the main themes of Heschel's religious thought is "the ineffable," a term that recalls the first of William James' four marks of mystical experience, "ineffability."

"Religion begins with the sense of the ineffable," Heschel declares. When we become aware of the ineffable we discover that "all existence is embraced by a *spiritual presence*," and that there is "a holiness that hovers over all things," making them appear to us "in some moments like objects of transcendent meditation, as if *to be* meant *to be thought of* by God. . . ." Thus we are led to affirm the existence of God.

Heschel calls this way of affirmation "the approach through the ineffable."[29] He also terms it "depth theology." "The theme of theology," he explains, "is the content of believing; the theme of depth theology is the act of believing, its purpose being to explore the depth of faith, the substratum out of which belief arises." It is concerned, he goes on to say, with "the miracle" of "the illumination of the soul." Depth theology "draws upon that which happens to man in moments of confrontation with ultimate reality. It is in such moments that decisive insights are born." Some of these insights may be conceptualized, but others must be conveyed in a language compatible with man's "sense of the ineffable."[30]

Again, the mystical implications of all this seem obvious. Would Rufus Jones have found in it anything to which he would object? The reference to insight may remind us of William James' second mark of mystical experiences—their "noetic quality." "They are states of insight into depths of truth unplumbed by the discursive intellect." Or we might note what Bertrand Russell has to say on this point. He remarks that "mystical philosophy, in all ages and in all parts of the world, is characterised by certain beliefs," and that the first of these is "the belief in insight as against discursive analytic knowledge."[31] Now, Heschel does not leave anyone in doubt that insight, not rational speculation, is his approach to God. In *Man Is Not Alone* he writes: "In thinking on the level of the ineffable, we do not set out with a preconceived idea of a supreme being in our possession, trying to ascertain whether He is in reality the way He is in our minds. The awareness which opens our minds to the existence of a supreme being is an awareness of reality, an awareness of a divine presence. Long before we attain any knowledge about His *essence*, we possess an intuition of a divine presence."[32] And in *God in Search of Man* he again states: ". . . understanding for the realness of God does not come about by way of syllogism, by a series of abstractions, by a thinking that proceeds from concept to concept, but by way of insights. The ultimate insight is the outcome of *moments* when we are stirred beyond words, of instants of wonder, awe, praise, fear, trembling and radical amazement. . . ."[33]

Once religious faith has been born in this manner, Heschel does not propose to exclude it from reason. Though he declares that "reason is not the measure of all things" and that faith does not "depend for its validity upon justification by science," he also affirms, "Truth has nothing to fear from reason. What we abhor is presumptuousness that often goes with super-rationalism, reason conditioned by conceit, reason subservient to passion." He then concludes: "Neither reason nor faith is all-inclusive nor self-sufficient. The insights of faith are general, vague and stand in need of conceptualization in order to be communicated to the mind, integrated and brought to consistency. Reason is a necessary coefficient of faith, lending form to what often becomes violent, blind and exaggerated by imagination. *Faith without reason is mute; reason without faith is deaf.*"[34]

Thus Heschel views reason as integral to his religious thought, but at the same time, like the famous mystics cited in Chapter I, like other mystics of world history whom Bertrand Russell had in mind, accords first priority to insight. I have already suggested that the "moments" from which he derives his decisive religious insights might well be regarded as mystical experience. It remains to inquire how he interprets that experience.

As one would expect, he interprets it in terms of the Conservative Judaism of which he is a leading exponent. For Heschel, God is the One God of Israel, of the prophets. He is "in search of man." Unlike "the God of the philosophers who is all indifference, too sublime to possess a heart or to cast a glance at our world," as Heschel puts it, He is "all concern, too merciful to remain aloof to His creation." The prophets have expressed this concern as God's anger, mercy, love. Heschel calls it "the divine *pathos.*"[35]

Man responds to God's intimate concern through prayer and also, Heschel emphasizes, through deeds, through moral action. For "the God of Israel has a passion for righteousness." He commands that man be righteous in his every act, in the common, everyday deeds no less than in the heroic ones. "The quest for right living," therefore, "is the authentic core of Jewish religion. It has been the main theme of Jewish literature," says Heschel, "from the prophets till the times of the Hasidim. . . ." The stress that Hasidism places upon right living has also been noted by Heschel's friend Martin Buber, who remarks that the teachings of Hasidism "can be summed up in a single sentence: God can be beheld in each thing and reached through each pure deed."[36]

Time, in Heschel's interpretation, has far greater value than it often receives in mystical thought—Meister Eckhart's, for instance. From Huxley's *Perennial Philosophy*, Heschel quotes Eckhart's dictum that "there is no greater obstacle to God than time" in order to disapprove of it. His own view is that, to Judaism, time is sacred. "Judaism is *a religion of history, a religion of time,*" he declares. "The God of Israel was not found primarily in the facts of nature. He spoke through events in history."[37]

Thus Heschel builds the edifice of his religious thought from foundation stones of Judaism. And when he writes mysticism it is Jewish mysticism, with that special emphasis upon the nearness of God and the profound holiness of everyday living which is so characteristic of the Hasidic tradition in which he was nurtured.

No less distinctive, in its way, is the mysticism that Merton presents from the viewpoint of the contemplative tradition in Catholicism. Like Heschel and Thurman, he became known to a wide reading audience in America about the middle of the century. In 1949, the year that Thurman published *Jesus and the Disinherited,* Merton's autobiography *The Seven Storey Mountain* (1948) rose to the upper brackets of best-seller lists throughout the United States. Merton was already an established poet, having published three volumes of free verse that had made him a favorite of the avant-garde. But now he reached not the few but the many. His richly detailed autobiography had the cumulative force of a novel. It was the story of his spiritual pilgrimage from a godless boyhood through worldly intellectualism to Catholicism and the contemplative life of a Trappist monk.

He was born in Prades, France, in 1915 to an American mother and an artist from New Zealand, Owen Merton, who painted landscapes "like Cézanne." When he was a year old his parents moved to America, settling in Flushing, Long Island. When he was six, his mother died of cancer, and afterward young Thomas lived a rootless life, traveling abroad with his father, attending school first in Bermuda, then in France, and finally in England, where he prepared for college at Oakham. In the summer of 1930 his father died of a malignant brain tumor, and he was left to the care of an English guardian and his American grandparents, who lived in Douglaston, Long Island. After a year at Cambridge he went to live with his grandparents and study at Columbia University, where he received his bachelor's degree in 1938 and his master's in English literature the following year.

Columbia was intellectually stimulating, and he not only did well in his classwork but also excelled in extracurricular activities as a student writer and editor. Yet his undergraduate years, by his own account, were spiritually stultifying. Neither the Freudian psychology that he read nor the communism in which he dabbled gave meaning to his existence, and long hours in New York night clubs, smoking and drinking and listening to jazz, only made matters worse. There came a time when he neared physical collapse and thought of suicide.

Instead he turned hesitantly, haltingly, but with ever increasing fervor to a mystical Catholic faith. Though his family religious background was Protestant, to the extent that it was religious at all, the impulse toward Catholicism seemed to be an irresistible leaven within him. Perhaps it went back to the church spires in the cathedral towns of his boyhood in southern France, and to the pious frescoes and mosaics that he had found so fascinating during hs student holidays in Rome. Certainly it was strengthened by the Catholic philosophers whom he had formed the habit of reading, and by William Blake, on whom he wrote his master's thesis. Blake, in addition, helped to incline him toward mysticism. So also did Aldous Huxley, with his advocacy of mysticism in his *Ends and Means.* Moreover, there were friends who encouraged both his mystical and his Catholic proclivities. In November, 1938, he was baptized in the Catholic Church.

In the months that followed his religious life intensified, and in the spring of 1940 he had a mystical experience. It happened in the Church of St. Francis in Havana, where he had gone to vacation and recuperate from an appendectomy. In the church also, before the altar, were row upon row of Cuban children, taking Communion. Suddenly in one glad shout they began the Creed, *"Creo en Diós...,"* and Merton became aware, as never before, of all that God meant to him:

> But what a thing it was, this awareness: it was so intangible, and yet it struck me like a thunderclap. It was a light that was so bright that it had no relation to any visible light and so profound and so intimate that it seemed like a neutralization of every lesser experience.
> And yet the thing that struck me most of all was that this light was in a certain sense "ordinary"—it was a light (and this most of all was what took my breath away) that was offered to all, to everybody, and there was nothing fancy or strange about it. It was the light of faith deepened and reduced to an extreme and sudden obviousness.
> It was as if I had been suddenly illuminated by being blinded by the manifestation of God's presence.

So Merton described the experience years later, in his autobiography, and reflecting further upon it he wrote:

> The reason why this light was blinding and neutralizing was that there was and could be simply nothing in it of sense or imagination. When I call it a light that is a metaphor which I am using, long after the fact. But at the moment, another overwhelming thing about this awareness was that it disarmed all images, all metaphors, and cut through the whole skin of species and phantasms with which we naturally do our thinking. It ignored all sense experience in order to strike directly at the heart of truth, as if a sudden and immediate contact had been established beween my intellect and the Truth Who was now physically really and substantially before me on the altar. But this contact was not something speculative and abstract: it was concrete and experimental

and belonged to the order of knowledge, yes, but more still to the order of love.

Another thing about it was that this light was something far above and beyond the level of any desire or any appetite I had ever yet been aware of. It was purified of all emotion and cleansed of everything that savored of sensible yearnings. It was love as clean and direct as vision: and it flew straight to the possession of the Truth it loved. . . . It lasted only a moment: but it left a breathless joy and a clean peace and happiness that stayed for hours and it was something I have never forgotten.[38]

Even before this experience he had decided that he wanted to be a priest. He all but entered a Franciscan monastery, but fell into tormenting doubts about his fitness for the priesthood and withdrew his application, after which he took a position teaching English at St. Bonaventure College during the academic year 1940–41. By now he was reviewing books for the *New York Times* and the *Herald Tribune,* and he had begun writing poetry and ambitious, unpublished novels. Still he could not lose the desire to be a priest, to enter a monastery, perhaps of a stricter order than the Franciscans; perhaps, he felt, he should enter the Cistercian Order of the Strict Observance, commonly known as the Trappists. During Easter Holy Week, 1941, he made a religious retreat at a Trappist monastery, the Abbey of Our Lady of Gethsemani, at Bardstown, Kentucky. In November he reached a firm decision: he would, if admitted, become a postulant at Gethsemani. Very soon afterward he received notice that he might be drafted into the army, for in those tense weeks the nation was close to war. He wrote his draft board, which granted him time to see whether he could be accepted as a postulant. In December, just after Pearl Harbor, he was admitted to the contemplative life.

He remained at Gethsemani until his death in 1968, being ordained a priest in 1949 and serving as Master of Novices from 1955 to 1965. Although in the monastery he was Father M. Louis, his many books went out to the world under his secular name, Thomas Merton. These volumes of poetry and prose, produced because writing was assigned to him as one of his monastic duties, deal primarily with religious themes but also with a great variety of secular topics, including much sharp criticism of totalitarianism, war, the American business ethos, and racial injustice.

Mysticism is, of course, a recurrent theme. The silent, ascetic, contemplative life of the Trappists is treated historically in *The Waters of Siloe* (1949) and *The Silent Life* (1957). It is revealed autobiographically in the final chapters of *The Seven Storey Mountain* and in Merton's personal journal, *The Sign of Jonas* (1953). In *The Ascent to Truth* (1951) Merton examines the mystical doctrine of St. John of the Cross, and in *Mystics and Zen Masters* (1967) he compares Christian mysticism with Zen. One of his most deeply felt works is the series of reflections on the spiritual life that he published as *Seeds of Contemplation* (1949). Its importance in his mystical thought is indicated by the fact that he wrote two sequels to it, *No Man Is an Island* (1955) and *Thoughts in Solitude* (1958), and then incorporated the original reflections in a fuller treatment, *New Seeds of Contemplation* (1961), a book which presents the essence of his mysticism as it developed through the years.

In none of these writings does Merton attempt to propound original theology. Rather, he emphasizes the fact that his views of the Trinity, Christ, Mary the Virgin Mother of God, and the other concepts of his faith harmonize with traditional Catholic doctrine. Similarly, he derives his approach to mystical experience from the long contemplative tradition in Catholicism. Like St. John of the Cross he writes of the need for faith, ascetic self-discipline, detachment, and loss of the ego. And like the great Carmelite and so many other mystics, he holds that ultimate truth is found, not by the speculative thinker, but by the seeker who climbs spiritual heights to God. In striving to communicate such truth as clearly and accurately as possible, one should be guided by the theologian, but "true contemplation"— that is, mystical experience—"is not arrived at by an effort of the mind. On the contrary, a man could easily lose his way in the forest of technical details which concern a professional theologian." But by the grace of God "true theologians," or mystics, apprehend

the Truth, not in distinct and clear-cut definitions but in the limpid obscurity of a single intuition that unites all dogmas in one simple Light, shining into the soul directly from God's eternity, without the medium of created concept, without the intervention of symbols or of language or the likenesses of material things.

Here the Truth is One Whom we not only know and possess but by Whom we are known and possessed. Here theology ceases to be a body of abstractions and becomes a Living Reality Who is God Himself.[39]

And here, the reader may feel, is an exposition of mystical experience which seems to stem not so much from reading and speculation as from memory. This autobiographical note, which sounds repeatedly in Merton's mystical writing, even when he does not use the first person singular, is the primary basis of its charm and persuasive power, and may go far toward explaining why his major literary efforts made his name known on several continents. Though he does not wear his mystical experience on his sleeve, he stands within the security of his contemplative order and is less reticent than either Thurman or Heschel when he writes of his inner spiritual life. We have seen how openly, in *The Seven Storey Mountain*, he described the mystical experience of his Cuban visit, and now we shall notice further examples of his personal testimony as we consider the central concept of his mystical thought, which is love.

Not *eros*, of course, but in Merton's words "the divine *agape* . . . charity which is the very nature of God." This is the love that Merton knows when he says Mass and finds that it is "like swimming in the heart of the sun." It is the love that he and his brother monks feel for Christ and Mary and each other and all mankind as they worship together at Gethsemani. Bowed in their white robes "in the church's shadow," hidden "in cowls as deep as clouds," they lose all sense of time and place.

> For we are sunken in the summer of our adoration,
> And plunge, down, down into the fathoms of our
>   secret joy
> That swims with indefinable fire.[40]

This love lies at the heart of mystical union: "the essence of that union is a pure and selfless love that empties the soul of all pride and annihilates it in the sight of God, so that nothing may be left of it but the pure capacity for Him." This love is the beginning, the duration, and the end. Let us follow Merton through one last intimate evocation of mystical experience, noticing how divine love encompasses the light and the darkness, the emptiness, the joy, and the peace.

He begins:

Compared with the pure and peaceful comprehension of love in which the contemplative is permitted to see the truth not so much by seeing it as by being absorbed into it, ordinary ways of seeing and knowing are full of blindness and labor and uncertainty.

The sharpest of natural experiences is like sleep, compared with the awakening which is contemplation. . . . Our souls rise up from our earth like Jacob waking from his dream and exclaiming: "Truly God is in this place and I knew it not!" God himself becomes the only reality, in Whom all other reality takes its proper place—and falls into insignificance.

Although this light is absolutely above our nature, it now seems to us "normal" and "natural" to see, as we now see, without seeing, to possess clarity in darkness, to have pure certitude without any shred of discursive evidence, to be filled with an experience that transcends experience and to enter with serene confidence into depths that leave us utterly inarticulate. . . . A door opens in the center of our being and we seem to fall through it into immense depths which, although they are infinite, are all accessible to us; all eternity seems to have become ours in this one placid and breathless contact.

God touches us with a touch that is emptiness and empties us. . . . All variety, all complexity, all paradox, all multiplicity cease. . . . the function of this abyss of freedom that has opened out within our own midst, is to draw us utterly out of our own selfhood and into its own immensity of liberty and joy. . . .

It is useless to think of fathoming the depths of wide-open darkness that have yawned inside you, full of liberty and exultation.

They are not a place, not an extent, they are a huge, smooth activity. These depths, they are Love. And in the midst of you they form a wide, impregnable country.

There is nothing that can penetrate into the heart of that peace. Nothing from the outside can get in. There is even a whole sphere of your own activity that is excluded from that beautiful airy night. The five senses, the imagination, the discoursing mind, the hunger of desire do not belong in that starless sky.[41]

Peace and joy, in divine love. We know that Thurman and Heschel would agree. The varieties of mysticism share striking similarities, not only within the Judaeo-Christian tradition but also, as we initially noted, within the broader context of West and Far East. The Far East now claims our attention, as we consider Oriental forms of mysticism that have taken root in America.

CHAPTER 5

Vedanta

In the *Varieties*, William James illustrated his comments on Vedanta with quotations from the published addresses of Swami Vivekananda. This was appropriate, for Vivekananda had gained international fame in the nineties as India's Vedanta emissary to the West. The dynamic monk, a member of the Ramakrishna Order, combined in his magnetic personality the poise of the contemplative with the drive of the man of action. He first came to the United States in 1893 as a delegate to the Parliament of Religions at the World's Columbian Exposition in Chicago, where his bold oratory electrified large audiences and launched him upon national lecture tours, which lasted until 1895 and were resumed during a second visit, 1899 to 1900. To many Americans the forceful swami in ocher turban and orange silk robe must have personified concepts of Oriental mysticism that they had previously encountered only in the pages of Emerson and his fellow transcendentalists.

Vivekananda has exerted a lasting influence upon mystical thought in America. From his lectures and organizational work of the nineties stems the present-day Vedanta movement in the United States, with its ten centers in Boston, New York, Los Angeles, and other cities, and its affiliation with the Ramakrishna Order, which has over a hundred centers in India and the rest of Asia, and one each in England, France, and Argentina.[1]

The American centers are devoted to the study and practice of Vedanta philosophy and religion, and are led by resident swamis trained in India by the Ramakrishna Order. In the twentieth century the swamis with literary proclivities have published translations from the sacred writings of India, biographies of Indian saints, and original interpretations of Indian thought. The growing audience for mystical ideas has been further widened by the publications of well-known authors like Aldous Huxley, Gerald Heard, and Christopher Isherwood who have associated themselves with the Los Angeles, or Hollywood, center.

"What is Vedanta?" asks Isherwood. He answers that it is "the philosophy of the Vedas," and more. "More generally speaking, the term 'Vedanta' covers not only the Vedas themselves but the whole body of literature which explains, elaborates and comments upon their teaching, right down to the present day." In terms of Indian philosophy, Vedanta, as it is taught and practiced in the American centers, embraces such mainstreams of Hindu thought as the Vedantic nondualism (*advaita* Vedanta) of Shankara and the Yoga of Patanjali.[2] The ideas which might be said to form its mystical core are set forth in two comprehensive books, *The Spiritual Heritage of India* (1963), by Swami Prabhavananda of the Hollywood center, and *Hinduism: Its Meaning for the Liberation of the Spirit* (1958) by Swami Nikhilananda of New York. Fundamental is the idea that God is both transcendent and immanent. God transcendent, called Brahman, is absolute existence, knowledge, and bliss, beyond space, time, and causation, beyond the reach of finite sense experience. God immanent, called Atman, dwells within man as his real Self, or soul. Brahman and Atman are the one God: " 'Brahman and Atman are one.' "[3] Like the great Christian mystics of Europe, like the Quakers from George Fox to Rufus Jones, Vedanta declares that man is a bodily temple in which divine spirit dwells.

It is extremely difficult for man to know his real Self because it is veiled from him by maya, the phenomenal world of appearance, which includes his own body, mind, and ego, with which he mistakenly identifies himself. Yet the whole purpose of his existence is to seek and find the Atman; and he is driven to this quest by the inescapable fact that in the phenomenal world he cannot attain lasting peace and happiness. The world affords him what Vedanta calls the pairs of opposites: good and evil, pleasure and pain, joy and suffering—a pattern of flux, of constant change. Eventually he wearies of all this and turns to God.

For individual man, this turning from the world to God is not the process of one lifetime, but of many lives. Vedanta incorporates the doctrine of karma and reincarnation. The individual is born, dies, and is reborn again and again, and his condition in each life is shaped by his karma, the cumulative effects of all his previous impulses, feelings, thoughts, words, and deeds. Karma, though powerful, does not entirely eliminate free will. "Indian philosophy is at no time, or in any sense, fatalistic," writes Prabhavananda. "The will as conceived by the Upanisads, and other Indian scriptures, has in it an element of complete freedom, a power sufficient to enable a man to act in direct opposition to the spontaneous tendency of his accumulated character—and therefore to control his future."[4]

In order to win freedom from the weary round of karma-fettered reincarnation, a man must rid himself of worldly desires, which act like magnets drawing him back to new births, and must penetrate the veil of maya and realize that his true, indwelling Self is one with God—"That thou art," in the profoundly simple Vedic phrase. He must, in other words, attain mystical consciousness, samadhi, as the Hindus call it. This superconsciousness is Vedanta's ultimate goal. Its all-important fruit is salvation. In samadhi the seer transcends the senses, transcends reason, and gains a higher knowledge than any spoken or written words, including even the scriptures, can yield. He proves for himself, by direct experience, the truth of the scriptural assurance, "That thou art."

"There are two kinds of samadhi," writes Nikhilananda. In the one, the aspirant "retains consciousness of the individual soul, the body, and the world, and at the same time sees them all as permeated by Brahman. . . ." In the other, "the I-consciousness is totally obliterated, and there no longer remains any distinction between knower, knowledge, and the object of knowledge."[5]

In all this the resemblance to Christian mysticism seems evident. Both Christian and Vedantic seers affirm the divinity of man, his mission to find God, and his capability, while still in this world, of finding Him through direct, transcendent experience. The German philosopher and theologian Rudolf Otto, in his *Mysticism East and West,* has analyzed the striking similarities between the doctrines of Meister Eckhart and Shankara. It is of course possible to draw distinctions between the common mystical concepts of Vedanta and Christianity. Otto discerns differences as well as conformity in the ideas of God and the soul advanced by Eckhart and Shankara. And Charles Eliot, writing from the viewpoint of the British historian, points out in his *Hinduism and Buddhism* that "our words, God and soul, do not cover quite the same ground as the Indian words which they are used to translate."[6] Granting the cogency of such distinctions, one might still conclude that in the broad view the similarities between Vedantic and Christian mysticism outweigh the differences, though inevitably there will be inexact correspondence between Sanskrit and Western words, and diversity among religious doctrines developed in different lands and centuries, by men struggling to express the ineffable.

The similarities appear in method as well as doctrine. The Indian aspirant who strives to free himself of worldly desires seems close to the Purgative Way of the European mystics, and centuries before St. John of the Cross experienced his meditative raptures the Vedic seers were developing contemplative techniques of God-seeking called yoga. The many meanings of the word "yoga" are set forth in Mircea Eliade's comprehensive study, *Yoga: Immortality and Freedom.* From the Vedantist viewpoint Nikhilananda and Prabhavananda define the word as meaning union with God and the method of that union. They devote considerable space in their books to discussions of four forms of yoga as spiritual disciplines: bhakti yoga, seeking God through love for Him; karma yoga, the selfless performance of work; jnana yoga, knowledge of Brahman through philosophical discrimination; and raja yoga, Self-realization through controlling the mind and practicing concentration and meditation in accordance with an eight-stage process systematized by Patanjali.

These forms are not mutually exclusive. Indeed in the Bhagavad-Gita, the "Bible of India," God incarnate as Krishna advocates harmonious practice of all of them, and Vedantists revere the Gita and follow Krishna's teaching. When engaged in meditation, which is fundamental to yoga as spiritual discipline, they may assume the "lotus posture" of crossed and interlocked legs, or they may—especially if they are Westerners—simply sit upright in a chair, since the one essential of posture is an erect spine. Yoga meditative posture, it might be added, is far removed from the strenuous bends and twists of hatha yoga, which seeks to perfect the body, and still farther removed from extreme yogic practices of the kind stressed by Arthur Koestler in *The Lotus and the Robot.*

Since both Nikhilananda and Prabhavananda are Vedantist monks, whose vocation in America is to find God and help others to find Him in the mystical manner, it may be assumed that mysticism to them is personal experience as well as religious doctrine. In *Hinduism* and the *Spiritual Heritage* they do not write of their own mystical experience, but Prabhavananda does present, in his preface, this personal testimony.

My point of view is in one respect different from that of the Western scholar. I speak always as one born to the religious tradition of India, convinced of the profound truth of its essential message and familiar with its manifestations in the life of my people. Thus a religious phenomenon that to the Western scholar might well seem remote and merely curious, an item to be scientifically noted but not to be taken seriously—I refer to the transcendental consciousness—is to me a plain fact of supreme significance. I have dwelt in close association with most of the monastic disciples of Śrī Rāmakṛṣṇa, each of whom had attained that ultimate and blessed experience; and I have seen one of them, my spiritual master, Swami Brahmananda, living almost constantly—as a direct result of that experience—in a state of ecstatic communion with God.[7]

Not only does this statement testify to the reality of the mystical experience; it sets forth, implicitly, the Vedic concept of the guru, a word that Prabhavananda might have used in place of the phrase "my spiritual master." The guru is a spiritual teacher who instructs his disciples out of knowledge gained partly from books but primarily from his mystical communion with God. Hence the disciple reveres his guru as no ordinary teacher but as a channel of the divine will.

At times, the Hindus believe, God undertakes the direct instruction and enlightment of mankind by incarnating as an avatar. According to Vedantists, Krishna and Buddha were avatars. So also was Christ. To exponents of Vedanta in the United States the mystical Vedic concepts are the keys that unlock the inner meanings of Christ's teachings. In the *Hindu View of Christ* (1949) Swami Akhilananda of the Vedanta Society of Boston argues that Jesus was an avatar and a yogi who emphasized bhakti yoga as the way to God. In *The Sermon on the Mount According to Vedanta* (1964) Prabhavananda also interprets the teachings of Jesus in terms of yoga. Christ's "birth in spirit to attain the Kingdom of God" he identifies with samadhi.[8]

In the introduction to his *Sermon on the Mount* he describes a personal mystical experience that occurred on Christmas Eve, 1914, in a monastery of the Ramakrishna Order near Calcutta, during the monks' annual special worship of Jesus.

Many of Sri Ramakrishna's disciples attended the service, among them my master, who was the president of our order. While we were seated in silence, my master said: "Meditate on Christ within, and feel his living presence." An intense spiritual atmosphere pervaded the worship hall. Our minds were lifted up, and we felt ourselves transported into another consciousness. For the first time I realized that Christ was as much our own as Krishna, Buddha, and other great illumined teachers whom we revered. As a Hindu, I was taught from childhood to respect all religious ideals, to recognize the same divine inspiration in all the different faiths. Thus Christ as a manifest expression of divinity I could never have considered foreign. But for a living and personal experience of him I needed the tangible heightening of consciousness resulting from the worship on that memorable Christmas Eve.[9]

Just as Krishna, Buddha, and Christ were avatars, so also, according to Vedanta, was Ramakrishna, the Indian saint who during his lifetime (1836–1886) practiced successively the spiritual disciplines of all the Hindu sects and of Christian and Moslem meditation and prayer, attesting that he found each of these varied paths a true way to God-realization. Vedanta's emissary to America, Vivekananda, was Ramakrishna's leading disciple and the chief founder of the Ramakrishna Order. Hence the concept of Ramakrishna as avatar is intrinsic to Vedanta in the United States. Yet the idea, as Isherwood has pointed out, is not dogma to be accepted in blind faith; for Vedanta, with deep roots in philosophical disputation, welcomes the honest questioner. In his widely read biography, *Ramakrishna and His Disciples* (1959), Isherwood declares his own faith in less than absolute terms. "I myself am a devotee of Ramakrishna; I believe, or am at least strongly inclined to believe, that he was what his disciples declared that he was: an incarnation of God upon earth."

As an exponent of Vedanta, Isherwood, since his removal to America from England in 1939, has written or edited a number of books and essays designed to popularize at a high level of scholarly integrity the main ideas of his religious philosophy. He is also interested in Quakerism. "The Society of Friends," he writes, "is, as far as I am aware, the Christian sect which comes closest to agreement with the teachings of Vedanta. The Friends believe that a religious life can only be lived by constantly meditating upon and recollecting the presence of an 'Inner Light' within the heart. This Inner Light is what the Hindu would call the Atman, the Reality within the individual. Like the Atman, the Inner Light is impersonal; though it may in practice be regarded by nearly all Quakers as the light of Christ's teachings."[10]

Quaker and Vedantic mysticism underlie several scenes in

Isherwood's novel, *The World in the Evening* (1952). This is the story of the wealthy dilettante Stephen Monk, whose selfishness blights his two marriages, but who learns to see his faults, to forgive himself, and to look hopefully toward a "guided" future foreseen for him by a devout Quakeress, an old family friend whom he calls Aunt Sarah. The mystical scenes, involving persons whose religious awakening must struggle against agnosticism, are brief and understated. In one, Stephen lies in bed "in the almost mindless calm of first waking," while the "thousands of bits" that make up his past life are contemplated by an inner "consciousness that had no name, no face, no identity of any kind." Some of his past actions are shameful. "But consciousness wasn't ashamed, because consciousness wasn't I. . . . It knew no feelings, except the feeling of being itself; and that was the deepest, quietest, most mysterious kind of happiness." Such consciousness, it need hardly be added, closely resembles the Atman.

In another scene Stephen's invalid wife Elizabeth gains awareness of what again would seem to be the Atman when, all alone one evening, she is suddenly gripped by the thought that she is about to die. She writes her friend Mary Scriven, telling how the fear reduced her to "a terrified animal" and relating what followed. "It was then, Mary, that I suddenly knew what to do. I gathered the creature up into my arms, as it were, ever so gently, and nursed it, and soothed it. I don't really quite know what I mean by this, because I don't know exactly who the 'I' was, who did the nursing. . . . the doing of it made me feel, to an intense degree, the distinction between the physical part of me and the —oh dear, how I *hate* that word 'spiritual'!—let's call it the higher, or deeper will. I was two quite distinct people at that moment—that much I know—and one of them tended the weakness of its animal sister. . . ." She goes on in the letter to declare her faith in God—"or in my version of Him, which I prefer to call 'It.' At least, I'm sure now (I used not to be) that there's a source of life within me—and that It can't be destroyed. . . . every sparrow, and everything that ever was born, is part of It. I, like everything else, am much more essentially in It than in I."

Elizabeth, walking alone in the valley of the shadow, has found mystical truth. Stephen and Gerda Mannheim, a young refugee from Nazi Germany, experience this truth through their association with Aunt Sarah. One night while the two women are sewing together Gerda thinks of her husband, a war prisoner in Germany, and tears so blind her that she cannot see her needle. Sarah does not move, does not speak. But from her there slowly emanates a knowing and silent communication, a "stillness" that assures Gerda that no matter what may happen, to her husband or to her, all is well.

Stephen's glimpse of the mystical truth within Sarah is the culmination of the story. It occurs on a sunny morning in her home near Philadelphia, just after she has told him that he will be guided, and that "Whatever you do, wherever you go—in the end it'll be all right." Stephen insists that she explain how she knows this. She answers that it cannot be explained "in so many words" but that she is "quite, quite sure." Stephen continues the narrative.

It was then, suddenly and for the merest fraction of an instant, that I saw, or thought I saw, what Gerda had seen. There was something about the smiling little woman, at that moment; something that wasn't the Sarah I'd known. That wasn't Sarah at all. The look in her eyes wasn't hers. I had an uncanny feeling—it was very close to fear—that I was somehow "in the presence"—but of what? The whatever-it-was behind Sarah's eyes looked out at me through them, as if through the eyeholes in a mask. And its look meant: Yes, I am always here.

I wanted to ask "what are you?" but I couldn't. I didn't dare admit that I had seen what I'd seen. That would be getting in too deep. The whatever-it-was was so vast that I daren't let myself go toward it. And, already, the instant had passed—before the clock could tick or the dust-motes move in the shaft of sunlight from the window.[11]

Thus once more Isherwood touches upon the timeless riddle of the inner Self, and again Vedantic mysticism finds expression in the novelist's art. Although such incidents as these are quantitatively but a fraction of *The World in the Evening,* they give it its deeper meaning and make it, essentially, a religious novel.

Vedanta is the main theme of *A Meeting by the River* (1967). In this short epistolary novel Isherwood dramatizes the conflict between two brothers; Oliver, who is about to take his final vows in a Hindu monastery on the Ganges, and Patrick, his charming, sybaritic elder, who visits the monastery and tries with unscrupulous ingenuity to tempt him back into the world. The necessity of dying to the false self is stressed by Oliver in a diary that he keeps, but of even greater importance to the working out of the plot is the concept of the guru and the mystical bond between guru and disciple. Oliver has been the disciple, in Munich, of a frail little swami who died before the young Englishman entered the monastery. When the temptations offered by Patrick become so great that Oliver fears he is about to abandon his religious goal he manages to hold to it by praying intensely to his departed guru. The result is a mystical experience of reunion with the swami, leading Oliver to reflect in his diary: "I knew that Swami was 'dead,' and I knew that nevertheless he was now with me—*and that he is with me always, wherever I am.*"[12] In this culminating episode, and especially in these words, Vedantic mysticism becomes the keystone of the novel.

Like Isherwood, his friends Heard and Huxley (who made their pilgrimage from England to America in 1937) have reached international reading audiences with numerous books exploring mystical ideas. Heard has advocated Vedanta in more than a few of the forty-seven volumes that he has published, chiefly in the fields of philosophy, history, science, and religion. "Most Westerners," he writes, "are looking for a religion that shall express and render to them an experience of the transcendent-immanent eternal life that physics has now deduced to be the nature of the universe. That Vedanta can give—all is Brahman: thyself art He."[13]

Within Vedanta, Heard includes the teachings of Buddha. His system of thought also embraces Christian mysticism and, indeed, mystical experience and ideas wherever and whenever they may be found in world history. All this he seeks to synthesize by means of his own version of emergent evolution. Presumably the writers who have influenced his evolutionary hypothesis include those whom he has named as advocates of the idea that life is a "hatching process"—Bergson, Hans Driesch, C. Lloyd Morgan, and others—but not Bucke, whose *Cosmic Consciousness* he does not mention.[14]

Like Bucke, Heard argues that man is still evolving, that he is emerging from the limits of self-consciousness into that heightened awareness which Bucke called "cosmic consciousness" and Heard identifies with mystical illumination, or samadhi. It is hardly an exaggeration to say that the bulk of Heard's factual writing is a massive marshaling of argument and evidence in support of this thesis, which is clearly set forth in the book that most fully expresses his mystical ideas, *Pain, Sex and Time*. Published in 1939, this study warns that civilization is in peril, and ascribes the menace of totalitarianism to the "mass neurosis" that has resulted from mankind's imprisonment in individual self-consciousness. Salvation lies in continuing evolution. That man has the reserve energy to continue is evidenced by his capacity to suffer pain and indulge in sexual pleasure. The nature of his continuing evolution must be not physical but psychical.

Unlike Bucke, Heard is not content to wait upon psychical evolution, letting illumination come to whom it will. Surveying the history of evolving consciousness from the Egyptians through the Hebrews, the Greeks, and the Middle Ages, he concludes that "there is an urge" within man "to dilate his awareness," and that effective methods of achieving this were developed by the more advanced medieval mystics, whose techniques are comparable to yoga. Man should now, he argues, further his psychical evolution by expanding his consciousness through yogic methods; proper diet, continence, and especially meditation. Society should be reorganized to achieve this all-important end—and Heard goes so far as to sketch his own Utopia, with centers of mystical teaching and practice, a cooperative economy, and an idealized Hindu caste system topped by advanced mystics or "Neo-Brahmins," selfless seers standing above nationalism and forming an "International Police Force."[15]

Heard restated this scheme in *Man the Master* (1942), but abandoned it in other books that develop his ideas on the evolution of consciousness and ways to achieve it. *The Creed of Christ* (1940) analyzes the Lord's Prayer as a ladder to mystical perfection. *The Code of Christ* (1941) presents a similar interpretation of the Beatitudes, pointing out their resemblance to "that other famous ascent to Understanding and Deliverance—the Eightfold Path of Buddha." In the *Creed* he suggests that Christ had evolved to so high a level of consciousness as to be "a new species," and that it is "man's task . . . to be so reborn as to become of that species." Christ "was the Son of Man, because, though greater than any of his generation, he was their junior, he was younger, he belonged, by the creative power which he allowed to keep flowing in renewal through him, to a generation of men who, even now after two thousand years, have yet to be born."[16]

In a later study, *The Eternal Gospel* (1946), Heard offers a variant of this idea. Christ manifested the power to redeem men from original sin—which Heard interprets in terms of karma-reincarnation—because, unlike ordinary beings, he had always succeeded in his spiritual evolution.

There could be a stock, stem or phylum of Life which from the beginning never failed. At every level, however rudimentary, it did exercise to the full its capacity for creative acceptance and never shrank back into rejection and self-insulation. Hence it would be radically free: Its physique would in no wise thwart its wish to act without restraint: It would never be ignorant of its real relationship to all its fellows and to the Eternal Life. Hence it would not only be mobilized wholly to serve others—they could come to salvation through it. For this power, to transcend the illusory but stubborn limitations of physique-personality, would make it possible for it to transfuse its vitality-consciousness into any who would accept this unique service.

Heard cites John 1:12: "As many as received him, to them gave he power to become the sons of God," and concludes, "This, too, is the Vedanta doctrine of the Avatar. . . ."[17]

The "exact translation" of the reference to evil in the Lord's Prayer, states Heard, is "Deliver us from The Evil." What is meant, he suggests, "is the evil of irresponsibility toward time," of postponing the effort to try now to find eternal life. Time and evil are closely linked in Heard's thought. His comment upon them can be found in a number of his books, including two not yet mentioned, *A Preface to Prayer* (1944), and *Is God in History?* (1950). Time, to Heard, is "illusion"—"that distortion and misapprehension under which individualized consciousness perceives reality." As the spiritual aspirant expands his consciousness and rises toward union with God in the Eternal Now, he gains freedom from time and also, Heard argues, from accidents, which occur only in time. Heard makes it clear that in coupling time with evil he is following Eckhart, and that he regards evil as the "supreme moral problem." Vedantic thinkers took the problem too lightly, he feels, when they explained evil as "due to God's 'play,' Lila," having "really . . . no actuality." This seems hardly to take account of the full intensity of evil as we encounter it in the unfriendly aspects of nature and in the malignancy that flaws the human heart (for Prabhavananda's view on this, see Appendix B). To redeem man from such intensity perhaps even God must suffer. Rather than the Vedantic resolution of the problem Heard prefers "the original Christian doctrine of the double nature and double will in Incarnation. The divine Redemptive Nature does not suffer, but the human nature that perfectly obeys the divine, does." Yet in the final analysis evil cannot be explained by rational argument, in terms that we can understand. Saints, by means of the mystical experience, may penetrate the riddle and see that all is well, but "they may not tell us in words why and how this is so and what in logical language evil is."[18]

The contemplative effort to achieve mystical experience is not, Heard insists, escapism. His stout defense of mystics against the charge that they are indulging in escapism runs through a number of his books. In *Pain, Sex and Time* he reverses the accusation, arguing that the true escapists are those who engage in constant work and social activities without ever facing the ultimate questions as to the meaning of life that the mystics seek to solve. In *The Source of Civilization* (1937) he equates yogic meditation with the practice of the research scientist who cloisters himself in order to carry on his effort to discover scientific truth. In *A Preface to Prayer* he defines prayer as "a method of empirical discovery, a technique for contacting and learning to know Reality," and advocates contemplation as "man's highest activity." The contemplative, expanding his consciousness toward unity with God, is "the growing point of evolution and the pioneer of humanity." As the still, silent tree cleanses the air of carbon dioxide, so does the contemplative purify the spiritual atmosphere.[19]

Heard's advocacy of mysticism—which is clearly that of a practicing contemplative—continued into the 1960's. In *The Five Ages of Man* (1963) the mystical ideas are somewhat muted, and overshadowed by an encyclopedic compendium of psychological and anthropological data, as Heard investigates the means by which mankind, in successive periods of world history, has sought psychological wholeness. Yet there is exposition of yogic method; the basic concept is the familiar thesis of evolving consciousness; and the ultimate goal of the author is the one that has inspired so many of Heard's books—the mystical experience.

Literary critics have tended to couple Heard's ideas with those of his friend Aldous Huxley, and to suggest that it was Heard who converted the famous novelist, in the 1930's, from skepticism to mysticism. Leaving to biographers the question of just how and when each thinker influenced the other, we may note that during their thirty-two-year friendship they shared interests in science, pacifism, Vedanta, Buddhism, and the mystical elements of Christianity and other religions. And in Los Angeles, where they settled in 1937, they found a teacher of Vedanta in Swami Prabhavananda.

Long before, in the 1920's, Huxley had begun publishing novels, short stories, and essays that showed a persistent interest in mysticism. By the mid-thirties he had moved from the religious position of a scientific-minded skeptic, through the "life-wor-ship" doctrine of D. H. Lawrence, to the beliefs of a scientific-minded mystic. He had expressed his mystical faith in his novel *Eyeless in Gaza* (1936) and in his philosophical study *Ends and Means* (1937). The meeting with Prabhavananda was another milestone. "This was a contact which had far-reaching effects on the lives of all three of us," says Isherwood. "In Huxley's case, it was widely represented as the selling-out of a once brilliant intellect. As a matter of fact, it actually enlarged Huxley's already vast intellectual horizons by introducing him to mystical experience as a fact, a phenomenon of existence." Heard recalls that Huxley not only wrote about yoga but "also set himself to test out and experiment with these traditional exercises." Huxley's own comment on his mystical practices was characteristically self-depreciating. "I came to this thing in a rather curious way, as a *reductio ad absurdum*," Isherwood recalls his remarking informally in 1942. "I have mainly lived in the world of intellectual life and art. But the world of knowing-about-things is unsatisfactory. It's no good knowing about the taste of straw-berries out of a book." What he was trying to do, he suggested, was to experience consciously the "spiritual reality" with which artists unconsciously "establish some contact" when they imprison beauty "within the white spaces between the lines of a poem, between the notes of music. . . . Now, obviously," he ended with quiet intensity, "one could never possibly give it up."[20]

Nor, until his death in 1963, did he ever give up trying in one way or another to taste spiritual reality. His efforts yielded what he himself regarded as modest results. Looking back on his experiences from the vantage point of May 1953, he felt that he had "known contemplation only in its humbler, its more ordinary forms"—for example, "as a rapt absorption in poetry or painting or music . . . as occasional glimpses, in Nature, of Wordsworth's 'something far more deeply interfused'; as systematic silence leading, sometimes, to hints of an 'obscure knowledge.' "[21] Like Rufus Jones, however, he augmented personal experience with historical investigation. After his meeting with Prabhavananda, he undertook an intensive study of the lives and teachings of outstanding mystics in the major religions. And the ideas thus derived from study and practice flowed into writings dominated by the mystical concern—into essays for the magazine *Vedanta and the West*, edited by Prabhavananda;[22] into the novels *After Many a Summer* (1939) and *Time Must Have a Stop* (1944); into the brilliant anthology, *The Perennial Philosophy* (1945), that stirred Rufus Jones; and into the historical studies, *Grey Eminence* (1941) and *The Devils of Loudun* (1952).

To encounter these ideas in all the variety of form and literary artistry with which Huxley expresses them is to gain a first impression of great diversity. But actually they tend to coalesce around three subjects that lie at the heart of mysticism: the nature of God, achieving union with God, and obstacles to union. Emergent evolution, so fascinating to his friend Gerald Heard, is not one of Huxley's major themes. But the scientific approach was a part of his personal make-up, as well as of his family heritage, and when he formulated his basic mystical beliefs he called them "The Minimum Working Hypothesis."

Under this title he published in *Vedanta and the West* a brief essay which he later used in *Time Must Have a Stop* as a part of the notebook kept by the aspiring mystic, Sebastian Barnack. As research in natural science needs a working hypothesis, so also, the essay suggests, does religious research into "purely spiritual reality." In natural science, when there is no working hypothesis, research lacks proper motivation and guidance. "Contrariwise, too much working hypothesis means finding only what you *know*, dogmatically, to be there and ignoring all the rest." The same is true of religion. For religious research, then, the minimum working hypothesis would seem to be about as follows:

That there is a Godhead or Ground, which is the unmanifested principle of all manifestation.
That the Ground is transcendent and immanent.

That it is possible for human beings to love, know and, from virtually, to become actually identified with the Ground.

That to achieve this unitive knowledge, to realize this supreme identity, is the final end and purpose of human existence.

That there is a Law or Dharma, which must be obeyed, a Tao or Way, which must be followed, if men are to achieve their final end.

That the more there is of I, me, mine, the less there is of the Ground; and that consequently the Tao is a Way of humility and compassion, the Dharma a Law of mortification and self-transcending awareness.[23]

The nature of God as here conceived is clearly evident. He is the ultimate God-without-form of Meister Eckhart and Vedanta, and of all high mysticism. Huxley did not rule out God-with-form, as manifested, for example, in the Christian Trinity of Persons and the Vedic concept of the avatar. But in *Ends and Means* he had concluded that the ultimate discovery of the mystical quest is not a personal but an impersonal God, and he affirmed this in *The Perennial Philosophy.*[24] The God of his working hypothesis is also both transcendent and immanent, both Brahman and Atman; and human beings can love Him, which implies that He also loves. Huxley elsewhere elaborates these ideas in terms of the invocation to the Lord's Prayer.

"Our Father which *art* in heaven." God is, and is ours—immanent in each sentient being, the life of all lives, the spirit animating every soul. But this is not all. God is also the transcendent Creator and Law-Giver, the Father who loves and, because He loves, also educates His children. And finally, God is "in heaven." That is to say, He possesses a mode of existence which is incommensurable and incompatible with the mode of existence possessed by human beings in their natural, unspiritualized condition. Because He is ours and immanent, God is very close to us. But because He is also in heaven, most of us are very far from God. The saint is one who is as close to God as God is close to him.

It follows that for unsaintly, unspiritualized men the achievement of union with God, "the final end and purpose of human existence," is no easy task. The sure means is meditation, and Huxley, like Heard, esteems the contemplative life superior to the life of action. This view, he points out, runs counter to modern pragmatic philosophy which "regards action as the end and thought as the means to that end." But it fully accords with "the Western mystical tradition," which holds that "action is safe only for proficients in the art of mental prayer." Even good works may distract spiritual beginners from God, and their good deeds may turn out not to be good after all. St. John of the Cross declares that such acts by well-intentioned persons without spiritual insight accomplish "little more than nothing, and sometimes nothing whatever, and sometimes even harm."[25]

Progress in the contemplative life entails mortification, dying to self. Huxley does not advocate severe physical austerities, and he condemns what might be called the pseudo mortification of the stern, stoical Puritan who practices such virtues as temperance and chastity while lacking humility and charity. "Mortification has to be carried to the pitch of non-attachment," he writes, "or (in the phrase of St. François de Sales) 'holy indifference'; otherwise it merely transfers self-will from one channel to another...." In other words, the aspiring mystic must learn to deny the thoughts and desires of the ego, must gradually die to the false self and realize the divine nature of his real Self, the Atman. In *The Perennial Philosophy,* Huxley quotes from the Chandogya Upanishad, "Rising above physical consciousness, knowing the Self as distinct from the sense-organs and the mind, knowing Him in his true light, one rejoices and one is free," compares this with William Law's declaration that salvation is "the life of God, or Christ of God, quickened and born again in you," and comments that what Law calls the new birth of God within the soul "is essentially the same fact of experience as that which the Hindus, two thousand and more years before, described as the realisation of the Self as within and yet transcendently other than the individual ego."[26]

We find God not only through self-naughting and meditation but also and preeminently through love. "God is love, and there are blessed moments when even to unregenerate human beings it is granted to know Him as love," writes Huxley. "But it is only in the saints that this knowledge becomes secure and continuous." Others must know Him "predominantly as law.... The law which we must obey, if we would know God as love, is itself a law of love. 'Thou shalt love God with all thy soul, and with all thy heart, with all thy mind and with all thy strength. And thou shalt love thy neighbor as thyself.' " To those who obey the law come what St. Paul termed the three fruits of the spirit, peace, love, joy. The unitive life is " 'more abundant,' " a life of "beatitude. Necessarily so; for the Brahman, who is one with the Atman, is not only Being and Knowledge, but also Bliss. . . ."[27]

In the most mystical of all his novels, *Time Must Have a Stop*, Huxley portrays a modern, everyday saint who obeys the law of love and whose knowledge of God has become secure and continuous. To worldly eyes Bruno Rontini is a foolish, insignificant bookseller, but he lives an inward life of beatitude. A conversation in his shop reminds him of the great saints of his religion, including Christ and Buddha, and the unitive life is kindled. "As he named them to himself, the little flame in his heart seemed to expand, as it were, and aspire, until it touched that other light beyond it and within; and for a moment it was still in the timeless intensity of a yearning that was also consummation."[28]

Doubtless Huxley would have been the first to admit that this sentence, for all its deft artistry, falls short of what he wishes to convey. He often commented on the inadequacy of language as a means of expressing mystical experience. In *After Many a Summer* his mouthpiece William Propter discourses on this problem, citing the ambiguity of the word "love." "Love on the human level means—what? Practically everything from Mother to the Marquis de Sade." It is doubly confusing when we press it into service on the transcendent level, as in the statement, "God is love." This amounts to "creating God in our own image." We should make a distinction between the human and the divine; ". . . we should say that we were in love, but that God was x-love. In this way, people who had never had any first-hand experience on the level of eternity would at least be given a chance of knowing intellectually that what happens on that level is not the same as what happens on the strictly human level."

Another aspect of the problem is that the word is not the thing but only its symbol. Psychologists who write of the mystical experience out of knowledge derived solely from verbal descriptions of it are like "professional aestheticians" who have "never been inside a picture gallery." Theologians, too, may mistake words for reality. Yet words must be used; despite the difficulties inherent in them, they are necessary. Mystics should use them as accurately and humbly as possible to "indirectly hint"—they can do no more—at the nature of their experience. Theologians should "work on the problem of finding the most adequate words in which to adumbrate the transcendent and inexpressible." In modern times "the language of spirituality" has declined in quality, and "lacking a proper vocabulary, people find it hard, not only to think about the most important issues of life, but even to realize that these issues exist. Words may cause confusion . . . but the absence of words begets a total darkness."[29]

Of all the words employed by the master craftsman Huxley in his writings on mysticism perhaps the one that recurs most often is "self." The troublesome ego becomes in his exposition the opposite of good, the substance of evil. "For the perennial Philosophy, good is the separate self's conformity to, and finally annihilation in, the divine Ground which gives it being; evil, the intensification of separateness, the refusal to know that the Ground exists." Since man has free will, he can of course choose self instead of God. But this will lead inevitably to suffering; for, as the Buddha so succinctly put it, "The cause of pain is the craving for individual life." It will lead, as Vedanta teaches, to the wheel of karma-reincarnation, to the colossal suffering and sorrow of the world. Is there a solution to the problem of evil? Huxley does not pose and answer the question directly. But he does point out that love can fathom "divine justice," and that the "pure in heart," when they penetrate the indescribable realm of eternity, can catch glimpses of the solution and "say, with Juliana of Norwich, that all shall be well. . . ."[30]

Like Gerald Heard, Huxley follows Eckhart in linking evil and the self with time. In *The Perennial Philosophy* he quotes Eckhart's ringing statement, "There is no greater obstacle to God than time." As Mr. Propter, he explains that God's kingdom, which the mystic experiences, is "timeless good," and that "nothing within time can be actual good." Time, to the mystic, is "the medium in which evil propagates itself." For the desires of the self corrupt all temporal acts, even those of supposedly selfless men, such as idealistic scientists. Every ideal, after all, is "merely the projection, on an enormously enlarged scale, of some aspect of personality." The only exception is "the ideal of liberation—liberation from personality, liberation from time and craving, liberation into union with God. . . ."[31]

In *Vedanta and the West* Huxley also wrote of time, calling attention to the stress laid upon the Eternal Now by Christ and all the great mystics, and—in a striking essay that later went into Sebastian's notebook—interpreting Hotspur's lines,

> But thought's the slave of life, and life's time's fool,
> And time that takes survey of all the world
> Must have a stop.

"Thought's enslavement to life is one of our favorite themes," comments Huxley. "Bergson and the Pragmatists, Adler and Freud," the dialectical materialists and the behaviorists— "all tootle their variations on it." But the twentieth century has paid scant attention to the rest of Hotspur's summary. "Life's time's fool. By merely elapsing time makes nonsense of all life's conscious planning and scheming." Though twentieth-century Americans and Europeans cling to a faith in Progress and "the bigger and better Future," they have seen their hopes mocked by totalitarianism and war. And, as the dying Hotspur knows so well, time does stop; and in that moment what matter temporal goals? Let us, therefore, suggests Huxley, choose the spiritual way. "It is only by taking the fact of eternity into account that we can deliver thought from its slavery to life. And it is only by deliberately paying our attention and our primary allegiance to eternity that we can prevent time from turning our lives into a pointless or diabolic foolery. The divine Ground is a timeless reality. Seek it first. . . ."[32]

Seek, and ye shall find; but not, Huxley reiterates, until you have overcome self. "The poet, the nature lover, the aesthete" may approach God by experiencing beauty in art or nature, but cannot go further without losing the ego. Wordsworth saw the mystical face of Nature but seems to have been content to put his feelings into poetry and to retain to the end his "enormous egotism." Thus he fell short of the unitive life. "If the poet remains content with his gift," Huxley sums up, "if he persists in worshipping the beauty in art and nature without going on to make himself capable, through selflessness, of apprehending Beauty as it is in the divine Ground, then he is only an idolater."[33]

An idolater, in Huxley's vocabulary, is a victim of self-love, no matter what form his idol takes; whether it be gross sensual indulgence, or Wordsworth's Nature, or the temporal scientific ideal decried by Mr. Propter, self-love is its pedestal. In this sense the Huxley novels might be described as veritable catalogs of idolatries. They are replete with hapless men and women who worship themselves through loveless sex, through art, science, scholarship, false religion, politics, social reform—the list from *Crome Yellow* (1921) to *Island* (1962) is almost as various as the content of Huxley's erudite mind. Among the idolaters in *Time Must Have a Stop* are Eustace and John Barnack, the uncle and father, respectively, of Sebastian. Eustace, an esthetic, cynical sensualist, dies of a heart attack, and then in a series of extraordinary chapters his disembodied consciousness is shown struggling against repentance and union with the Clear Light of the Void, finally choosing self instead of salvation. John, a vigorous, idealistic politician, never ceases to pursue social reform, but as the story ends Sebastian suddenly sees him as a frustrated sixty-five-year-old man whose faith in the future is belied by the second world war and its aftermath, and who has become grotesque simply by remaining what he has always been.[34] John Barnack's worldly life is time's fool.

More memorable as an example of political idolatry than any fictional character of Huxley's is Father Joseph (François Leclerc du Tremblay), confidant and adviser to Cardinal Richelieu. In his biographical study *Grey Eminence* Huxley concludes that this talented aristocrat turned ascetic Capuchin monk was a genuine mystic who was diverted into power politics by his royalist, nationalistic impulses, which caused him to conceive of France as the instrument of God. His vicarious ambition, sublimated into preoccupation with national power, led him to rationalize even his efforts to prolong the Thirty Years' War as doing God's will. In the end he stultifies his spiritual attainments. The wages of sin is death to the unitive life.

In the Huxley inventory, then, the obstacles to union with God are numerous, diverse, and potent. Since other writers, too, usually find sin easier to handle than virtue, it is hardly surprising that the ferocious satirist of *Antic Hay* and *Brave New World*, when he deals with mysticism, gives much attention to stumbling blocks and the follies of stumblers. But his mystical faith, it should be remembered, is that divine good shall ultimately prevail over evil. This faith shines through even the darkness of *The Devils of Loudun*, wherein, amid harrowing accounts of superstition and torture in seventeenth-century France, Huxley avers that Atman is Brahman and that the "urge to self-transcendence" rivals the "urge to self-assertion." He believes also that the urge to self-transcendence is aroused and augmented by "graces . . . the free gifts of help bestowed by God upon each one of us, in order that we may be assisted to achieve . . . unitive knowledge of divine reality." Such experiences may seem almost commonplace, or they may resemble the onset of "cosmic consciousness" described by Bucke. Whatever their nature, if the recipient responds as he ought, using his free will to overcome self, he will receive more grace, and so progress toward salvation.[35] Thus in its ultimate conclusions Huxley's thought is optimistic, in keeping with the positive outlook of Vedanta and of mysticism in general.

Optimism also characterizes Huxley's well-known experiments with psychedelic drugs. Since these experiments were non-Vedantist, and pertain to the controversy over drugs and mysticism, they will be considered in Chapter 7. They will further illustrate the scientific bent that is the hallmark of Huxley's approach to all religious questions. Of the major American writers who have advocated the religious philosophy that Vivekananda brought to the United States, it is Huxley who is preeminently the philosopher-scientist, more so than his fellow British pilgrim to the Hollywood center, Isherwood, more so even than that other scientific-minded pilgrim, Gerald Heard. All three, together with the swamis who have written books, have discussed their faith at the high intellectual level which is one of the chief characteristics of Vedantic thought in America. But their intellectual detachment should not be emphasized at the expense of the devotion that underlies their writings and is also very much a part of Vedanta. This religious philosophy has had its austerely logical Shankara, but also its intensely devotional Ramakrishna. Its thought and its love of God are not mutually exclusive, but reciprocal.

CHAPTER 6

Zen Buddhism

A distinguished participant in the Parliament of Religions at Chicago, where Vivekananda expounded Vedanta in 1893, was the Abbot Soyen Shaku of Engaku Monastery in Kamakura, Japan, "the first Zen personage to make his way to the West."[1] He did not speak English, he was overshadowed by the eloquent Vivekananda, and one might say that his undramatic visit typifies the beginnings of Zen Buddhism in the United States. For more than half a century, the exponents of Zen who came to America found relatively few Americans interested in this form of mysticism. It would have been a prescient prophet indeed who could have foretold that by the 1950's Zen would become an excitement in American intellectual circles and a subject of considerable interest to the mass audiences of press, radio, and television.

Yet the years before the fifties did witness certain significant developments. In this seedtime era, exponents of both Soto and Rinzai, the two living Zen sects of modern Japan, came to Hawaii and the West Coast cities and implanted their ways of mystical meditation. Soyen Shaku, who represented the Rinzai sect, followed his Chicago visit with a longer one in 1905–1906, working with a small group of followers in San Francisco, touring the eastern states, and meeting President Theodore Roosevelt. The speeches that he delivered during this sojourn were published in Chicago in 1906 as *Sermons of a Buddhist Abbot*, the first book to introduce Zen philosophy to America.[2]

The religious tone of the *Sermons* might surprise a present-day reader so imbued with secularistic interpretations of Zen that he would never imagine a Zen master speaking reverently of God. Soyen Shaku does so speak. In a typical passage he declares: ". . . the Buddha-intelligence is universal and works in every one of us to bring out the consciousness of oneness underlying all individual phenomena. We as individuals are all different. . . . But we must never lose sight of 'the same God that worketh all in all,' and 'in which we move and live and have our being,' for he is the source of eternal life and the fountain of love."[3] As we shall see, a similarly religious yet more impersonal philosophy characterizes the interpretations of leading Zenists of our own time.

After Soyen Shaku, three other exponents of Zen claim our attention—the monks Sokei-an Sasaki and Nyogen Senzaki, and the world-famous Buddhist scholar and lay theologian, Daisetz Teitaro Suzuki. Sokei-an Sasaki came from Japan in 1906 as one of a group of Zenists wishing to found an American monastery. After that effort failed, he remained in the United States, eventually settling in the city of New York. In 1919 he went back to Japan for further study of Zen, but returned in 1928 and two years later founded in New York the First Zen Institute of America, which he directed until his death in 1945. His writings in English were published in 1947 in a volume entitled *Cat's Yawn*, the name of a short-lived periodical that Sokei-an had issued, 1940–41.[4]

Nyogen Senzaki, having studied under Soyen Shaku and other teachers in Japan, came to the United States in 1905 and for many years lived in California as a religious wanderer and occasional lecturer on Buddhism. In 1931 he established in Los Angeles a nonsectarian Zen center, serving as its spiritual leader until he died in 1958. Several small books which he published with Paul Reps were combined in one volume entitled *Zen Flesh, Zen Bones* (1957).[5]

Suzuki, too, was a disciple of Soyen Shaku, and if that eminent Zen master had never visited the United States nor published his *Sermons* he would still have a place in the history of Zen in America because of his association with his brilliant student. For Suzuki, though he moved at first in his master's shadow, became in time the foremost interpreter of Zen Buddhism to America and the West, the thinker and teacher who almost single-handedly initiated the Zen excitement of the fifties in the United States.

Although he lived most of his long life (1870–1966) in his native Japan, he resided in America from 1897 to 1909 and again from 1949 to 1957. During his first stay he lived in La Salle, Illinois, and worked as translator, copy editor, and writer for the Open Court Publishing Company, a position for which he had been recommended by Soyen Shaku. He served as interpreter to Soyen Shaku during his teacher's American tour of 1905–1906, and afterward edited and translated into English the *Sermons of a Buddhist Abbot.*[6]

Following his return to Japan in 1909 he became a university professor, first of English and then of the philosophy of religion, resumed his study of Zen with Soyen Shaku, married an American, Beatrice Lane, and founded a periodical, *The Eastern Buddhist,* for which he wrote articles that later served as bases for his books. A prolific writer, he published during his long career about one hundred books in Japanese and some thirty in English. His cornerstone work in English consists of his three volumes of *Essays in Zen Buddhism,* published as First Series (1927), Second Series (1933), and Third Series (1934). Other important works are *Studies in the Lankavatara Sutra* (1930), *The Training of the Zen Buddhist Monk* (1934), *An Introduction to Zen Buddhism* (1934), *Manual of Zen Buddhism* (1935), *Zen Buddhism and Its Influence on Japanese Culture* (1938), and *Mysticism: Christian and Buddhist* (1957).

Suzuki's books earned him an international reputation. In 1936 he visited England, where he participated in the World Congress of Faiths and lectured on Zen at a number of universities, including Oxford and Cambridge. Then came a temporary eclipse. Japan entered the second world war, and Suzuki, who had no enthusiasm for it, waited for the bloodshed to end. After the war, the Buddhist Society of London undertook the publication of his Collected Works, and in 1949 the seventy-nine-year-old scholar began his second American career, lecturing at numerous universities from Hawaii to the Atlantic seaboard, and taking up residence in 1951 in New York, where he remained until 1957 as a professor of religion at Columbia University.[7] By the time he returned to Japan, in 1958, the American boom in Zen was well under way.

Suzuki's message to America in the fifties was essentially what he had been saying for years in his scholarly works. In these writings, published unsystematically over a period of many years and understandably not without a few inconsistencies, he occasionally expresses uncertainty about classifying Zen as mysticism.[8] But generally, like other authorities, he does present Zen Buddhism as mysticism, inspired by the "Supreme Perfect Enlightenment" that came to Gautama the Buddha one day in India in the sixth century B.C. as he serenely meditated in the lotus posture. From the teachings of the Enlightened One arose Buddhism, which branched into various sects as it slowly spread through Asia. Tradition has it that Zen, which is a sect of Mahayana Buddhism, reached China in the sixth century and Japan in the twelfth. In China it was influenced by Taoism and Confucianism. Suzuki suggests that it was the pragmatic Chinese who gave Zen the terse, matter-of-fact directness that is one of its distinctive marks.[9]

The Japanese term "Zen," he explains, derives from the Chinese word *Ch'an*, an abbreviation of *Ch'anna*, which in turn derives from the Sanskrit word *dhyana* meaning meditation—that is, the deep contemplation that leads to mysticial experience. Zen followers spend much time practicing *zazen*, which means sitting in meditation, in the lotus posture preferably, with the spine erect, the breath regulated, and the mind stilled.[10] The Zen master may also assign his student a spiritual problem called a *koan*. Meditating upon the koan, the student seeks to discover the truth it expresses. Rinzai Zen makes more use of the koan than does Soto, and Suzuki, as a follower of the Rinzai sect, has much to say about the koan exercise.

"A koan," he explains, "is generally some statement made by an old Zen master, or some answer of his given to a questioner." For example: "A monk asked, 'All things are said to be reducible to the One, but where is the One to be reduced?' Chao-chou answered, 'When I was in the district of Ch'ing I had a robe made that weighed seven *chin.'* "[11]

No amount of logical analysis will solve this koan, nor any other, Suzuki insists. The answer of the Zen master is the expression of an enlightened state of consciousness, beyond logic. To understand it, the student must, in the mystical manner, transcend logic and achieve enlightenment. Thus the koan functions as an aid to the attainment of this mystical experience—*satori*, as it is called in Japanese. Even so, the solution of a particular koan may require several years of intense meditative effort. Once the first satori has been attained and the first koan solved, the student finds that he can more readily solve other koans, expressing other aspects of Zen truth.[12]

Suzuki writes about satori with the zeal of the mystic, declaring it to be "the Alpha and Omega of Zen Buddhism. Zen devoid of satori is like a sun without its light and heat," he continues. "I want to emphasize this most fundamental fact concerning the very life of Zen; for there are some even among the students of Zen themselves who are blind to this central fact and are apt to think when Zen has been explained away logically or psychologically, or as one of the Buddhist philosophies which can be summed up by using highly technical and conceptual Buddhist phrases, Zen is exhausted. . . . But my contention is, the life of Zen begins with the opening of satori. . . ."[13]

This "most intimate individual experience" is ineffable. It "cannot be expressed in words or described in any manner. All that one can do in the way of communicating the experience to others is to suggest or indicate, and this only tentatively."[14] But fortunately Suzuki does not let these difficulties force him into silence. He has much to tell us about satori.

He views it as the ripe spiritual fruit of disciplined, moral living, of which the life of the Zen Buddhist monk, with its combination of manual labor and meditation and its ideals of poverty, humility, and inner sanctification, is the model. The fruit may be long in ripening; several years, at least, of patient, hard effort under the guidance of the Zen master may be necessary before satori comes. Then it may come quite unexpectedly, precipitated, perhaps, by a blow with a stick or a slap in the face; for Zen masters, according to the traditional stories that Suzuki loves to tell, have often communicated immediate awareness of reality to their disciples by using physical force on them. Consider for instance the story of the disciple Hyakujo and his master Baso, who went out one day and saw a flock of wild geese flying.

"What are they?" asked Baso.

"They are wild geese, sir."

"Whither are they flying?"

"They have flown away, sir."

Baso seized Hyakujo's nose and twisted it.

"Oh! Oh!" cried the pain-stricken disciple.

"You say they have flown away," said Baso, "but all the same they have been here from the very beginning."

Cold perspiration wet Hyakujo's back. He had satori.[15]

The viewpoint of mystical Oneness from which Baso spoke, and to which he dragged Hyakujo by the nose, will be discussed a bit later. The point here is that the old Zen masters could sometimes be harsh in their efforts to give their students enlightenment. The additional point, which Suzuki never pauses to explain because it seems to him so obvious, is that such harshness is only the tip of the iceberg. Infinitely more important than the sudden pain which blocks intellection and finally triggers satori is the long practice of right living and zazen that precedes it.

While the Soto school tends to emphasize the gradual attainment of mystical experience, Suzuki, writing from the Rinzai viewpoint, stresses the abrupt nature of satori. "All true mystics are followers of the 'abrupt' school," he declares. "The flight from the alone to the alone is not, and cannot be, a gradual process." When satori finally comes, it is like "a bolt of lightning," or "an explosion shaking the very foundations of the earth."[16] Or so Suzuki describes it in the first series of *Essays*. In the second series he is less dramatic and more analytical. In the manner of William James, he presents the "chief characteristics of satori":

1. *Irrationality.* By this I mean that satori is not a conclusion to be reached by reasoning, and defies all intellectual determination. Those who have experienced it are always at a loss to explain it coherently or logically. . . . The satori experience is thus always characterized by irrationality, inexplicability, and incommunicability.

2. *Intuitive insight.* That there is noetic quality in mystic experiences has been pointed out by James in his *Varieties of Religious Experience*, and this applies also to the Zen experience known as satori. . . . It is noteworthy that the knowledge contained in satori is concerned with something universal and at the same time with the individual aspect of existence.

3. *Authoritativeness.* By this I mean that the knowledge realized by satori is final, that no amount of logical argument can refute it.

4. *Affirmation.* What is authoritative and final can never be negative. . . . Though the satori experience is sometimes expressed in negative terms, it is essentially an affirmative attitude towards all things that exist. . . .

5. *Sense of the Beyond.* Terminology may differ in different religions, and in satori there is always what we may call a sense of the Beyond; the experience indeed is my own but I feel it to be rooted elsewhere. The individual shell in which my personality is so solidly encased explodes at the moment of satori. . . . my individuality, which I found rigidly held together and definitely kept separate from other individual existences . . . melts away into something indescribable, something which is of quite a different order from what I am accustomed to. The feeling that follows is that of a complete release or a complete rest— the feeling that one has arrived finally at the destination.

6. *Impersonal Tone.* Perhaps the most remarkable aspect of the Zen experience is that it has no personal note in it as is observable in Christian mystic experiences. There is no reference whatever in Bud-

dhist satori to . . . Father, God, the Son of God, God's child, etc. . . . Is this owing to the peculiar character of Buddhist philosophy? Does the experience itself take its colours from the philosophy or theology?

7. *Feeling of Exaltation.* That this feeling inevitably accompanies satori is due to the fact that it is the breaking up of the restriction imposed on one as an individual being, and this breaking up is not a mere negative incident but quite a positive one fraught with signification because it means an infinite expansion of the individual.

8. *Momentariness.* Satori comes upon one abruptly and is a momentary experience. In fact, if it is not abrupt and momentary, it is not satori.[17]

Such are the chief characteristics of satori as Suzuki sees them. He also tells us that "there is a gradation in satori as to its intensity." Later satoris, resulting from continuing zazen, may be more intense than the first. But ideally the first satori is not "lukewarm" but "a fiery baptism of the spirit," which, in the colorful Zen metaphor, transforms "a common cur" into "a golden-haired lion." This mystical experience should not be confused with autosuggestion, nor can it be regarded as "a morbid state of mind, a fit subject for abnormal psychology." On the contrary, it enhances morality and strength of character. After satori you remain "normal as ever," but you live a richer life. The world is more beautiful. "All your mental activities are now working to a different key, which is more satisfying, more peaceful, and fuller of joy than anything you ever had."[18]

This passage and others in Suzuki's writings—especially his discussion of the "sense of the Beyond"—seem to reflect his personal mystical experience. Though he is reticent when it comes to speaking explicitly of his own satori, he has occasionally commented on it. Once, it is said, when he was asked "how it feels to have attained satori" he replied, "Just like ordinary everyday experience, except about two inches off the ground!"[19] On another occasion he told how in 1896 he achieved *kensho* (the first satori) during the December *sesshin* (week of intense meditation) at Engaku monastery. It was the culmination of "four years of struggle, a struggle mental, physical, moral and intellectual," during which he had become so frustrated trying to solve the first koan that Soyen Shaku had given him that he often talked of suicide. He knew in 1896 that he was going to America, and he felt that the December meditation was his last chance.

"I must have put all my spiritual strength into that sesshin," he recalled.

About the fifth day, he experienced selflessness, oneness with the koan, mystical awakening—kensho. "I said, 'I see. This is it.' " He presented himself to Soyen Shaku and successfully answered all test questions on the koan but one, which he answered the following morning. "I remember that night as I walked back from the monastery to my quarters in the Kigenin temple, seeing the trees in the moonlight. They looked transparent and I was transparent too.

"I would like to stress the importance of becoming conscious of what it is that one has experienced," he added. "After kensho I was still not fully conscious of my experience. I was still in a kind of dream. This greater depth of realization came later while I was in America"—where doubtless he continued practicing zazen. After he had achieved the deeper realization, he "did not find passing koans at all difficult. Of course other koans are needed to clarify kensho, the first experience," he concluded, "but it is the first experience which is the most important. The others simply serve to make it more complete and to enable one to understand it more deeply and clearly."[20]

What effect did his mystical experiences have upon Suzuki? According to his friend and editor Christmas Humphreys, president of the Buddhist Society, London, they molded a notable character and personality. In his editor's foreword to the Collected Works, Humphreys wrote of Suzuki: "Though not a priest of any Buddhist sect, he is honoured in every temple in Japan, for his knowledge of spiritual things, as all who have sat at his feet bear witness, is direct and profound. When he speaks of the higher stages of consciousness he speaks as a man who dwells therein, and the impression he makes on those who enter the fringes of his mind is that of a man who seeks for the intellectual symbols wherewith to describe a state of awareness which lies indeed 'beyond the intellect.' "[21]

When Suzuki interprets the mystical experience of Zen he draws, as one would expect, upon the religious philosophy of Mahayana Buddhism. Indeed, as we have seen, he suggests that satori itself may possibly "take its colours" from Buddhist philosophy. A tradition of Zen, to be sure, is that it has no philosophy, its essence being summed up in these lines:

> A special transmission outside the Scriptures;
> No dependence upon words and letters;
> Direct pointing to the soul of man;
> Seeing into one's nature and the attainment of Buddhahood.[22]

But Suzuki makes it clear that while Zen does not officially enshrine any verbal teaching—cherishing, rather, an iconoclastic tradition—its followers nevertheless study Buddhist scriptures and interpret their mystical experience by means of Buddhist concepts.

Certain of these, deriving from the ancient Indian religion, are close to those of Vedanta. Zenists, like Vedantists—and, indeed, most of the peoples of the Far East—believe in karma and reincarnation, and seek freedom from the painful wheel of birth-and-death. It is ultimately to attain this freedom that they practice their right living and zazen, and seek satori. This mystical "seeing into one's nature" delivers the Zenist from the delusion of ego and reveals to him his true Self, the Buddha-nature within. Hence, like Vedanta, Zen might be described as a way of Self-realization. Moreover, the Zen master resembles the Vedantist guru in that ideally he is a man of deep mystical experience, the authenticity of which has been certified by his own master, the two of them forming links in a long chain of master-disciple relationships.

Suzuki, as we have noted, compares the mysticism of Zen not with Vedanta but with Christianity, remarking that satori is "impersonal"—unrelated in any way to the Christian concept of a personal God. Elaborating on this point he writes: "Satori is not seeing God as he is, as may be contended by some Christian mystics. Zen has from the very beginning made clear its principal thesis, which is to see into the work of creation and not interview the creator himself. The latter may be found then busy moulding his universe, but Zen can go along with its own work even when he is not found there. . . ."

"Zen," he continues, "wants absolute freedom, even from God." Its effort to be free from all limiting concepts accounts for its blunt saying, "Cleanse your mouth even when you utter the word 'Buddha.' " "It is not that Zen wants to be morbidly unholy and godless," explains Suzuki, "but that it knows the incompleteness of a name."[23]

If not God, what ultimate reality does the Zen mystic experience when he has satori? When Suzuki discusses that reality, what words does he use, what ideas does he express? He uses, synonymously, a number of terms, such as "Buddha-nature," "self-nature," "Suchness," and especially *sunyata*, "Emptiness," which is realized through *prajna*, intuitive wisdom. Western scholars, studying the Mahayana notion of Emptiness, or "Void," in the writings of the Indian philosopher Nagarjuna and his followers, have sometimes viewed it as nihilistic,[24] but Suzuki insists in the language of mystical paradox that on the contrary the sunyata doctrine hints at "an ultimate reality," an "Absolute Emptiness" transcending logic, time, and space, "a void of inexhaustible contents," which "holds in it infinite rays of light and swallows all the multiplicities there are in this world."[25]

In the Kegon school of Japanese Buddhism, which has influenced Zen thought, the idea of sunyata is elaborated in the doctrine of interpenetration. The world, viewed spiritually, is pure light. Everything in it is interpenetrating and mutually conditioning, each object being not only itself but also every other object. Thus "all things are one, and that one is the Supreme Reality."[26]

Because of his enlightened consciousness of this Oneness, Baso could affirm that the wild geese had not flown away. To such consciousness, the logical formula runs, "A is at once A and not-A," and almost any statement, however it may violate ordinary logic, is possible. In the homely language that Zen often uses, "When Mr. Chang drinks Mr. Li grows tipsy." In more poetic expression:

> Empty-handed I go and yet the spade is in my hands;
> I walk on foot, and yet on the back of an ox I am riding:
> When I pass over the bridge,
> Lo, the water floweth not, but the bridge doth flow.[27]

Suzuki does not fail to note that Western mystics also affirm Oneness. Indeed sunyata finds expression, he suggests, in the philosophy of Meister Eckhart, who declares that "God and Godhead are as different as active and inactive," and speaks of the Godhead in such terms as "still desert" and "nothingness." This notion of the Godhead, Suzuki suggests, is "in perfect accord" with the doctrine of Emptiness.[28]

Buddha-nature is of course synonymous with sunyata, since in the Mahayana philosophy all Buddhas, though infinite in number, are ultimately One, and that One is the Only Reality. Hence the Buddha-nature is in all; every man is Buddha; and every man is in Nirvana, the perfect spiritual freedom of Buddha, which is One with the everyday, phenomenal world. Yet, holds the Zenist, each man must not merely accept all this intellectually but realize it for himself in the mystical manner, as he follows the path to enlightenment.

One who has attained enlightenment, but has postponed the supreme enlightenment of fully perfected Buddhahood in order to keep a vow to help all beings attain spiritual freedom, is called a Bodhisattva. His heart overflows with compassion and love for all that lives. He is his brother's keeper; he knows that in Oneness he *is* his brother. "The Mahayana is preeminently the religion of the Bodhisattva," writes Suzuki, "and the Bodhisattva's life of devotion (*bodhisattvacaryā*) is the ideal of the Zen life."[29]

Such, then, in brief compass, is Suzuki's mystical message to the West. It is not likely that many Americans read the three volumes of *Essays,* but certain of the shorter works, such as *An Introduction to Zen Buddhism* and *Mysticism: Christian and Buddhist,* reached wider audiences, in both hardcover and paperback editions.

Those who did not learn of Zen from Suzuki could turn to Alan Wilson Watts, whose role as a leader in the Zen boom of the fifties was second only to that of the Japanese scholar. Watts, an English editor and author, immigrated in 1938 to the United States, where he has been, successively, a theological student, an Episcopal priest and chaplain, a college professor and dean, and, since 1957, an independent writer and lecturer. In an autobiographical essay, "This Is It," he has described two experiences which he had at unspecified times (but evidently early in his career) and which he regards as mystical. In the essay he applies to them Bucke's phrase, "cosmic consciousness."

Shortly after I had first begun to study Indian and Chinese philosophy [he writes of the first experience], I was sitting one night by the fire, trying to make out what was the right attitude of mind for meditation as it is practiced in Hindu and Buddhist disciplines. It seemed to me that several attitudes were possible, but as they appeared mutually exclusive and contradictory I was trying to fit them into one—all to no purpose. Finally, in sheer disgust, I decided to reject them all and to have no special attitude of mind whatsoever. In the force of throwing them away it seemed that I threw myself away as well, for quite suddenly the weight of my own body disappeared. I felt that I owned nothing, not even a self, and that nothing owned me. The whole world became as transparent and unobstructed as my own mind; the "problem of life" simply ceased to exist, and for about eighteen hours I and everything around me felt like the wind blowing leaves across a field on an autumn day.

The second experience came "a few years later . . . after a period when I had been attempting to practice what Buddhists call 'recollection' (*smriti*) or constant awareness of the immediate present. . . ." Discussing this with him one evening, someone suggested that there was no need for such effort, since "we are always completely *in* the present" regardless of our thoughts. "This, actually quite obvious, remark again brought on the sudden sensation of having no weight," says Watts.

At the same time, the present seemed to become a kind of moving stillness, an eternal stream from which neither I nor anything could deviate. I saw that everything, just as it is now, is IT—is the whole point of there being life and a universe. I saw that when the *Upanishads* said, "That art thou!" or "All this world is Brahman," they meant just exactly what they said. Each thing, each event, each experience in its inescapable nowness and in all its own particular individuality was precisely what it should be, and so much so that it acquired a divine authority and originality. It struck me with the fullest clarity that none of this depended on my seeing it to be so; that was the way things were, whether I understood it or not, and if I did not understand, that was IT too. Furthermore, I felt that I now understood what Christianity might mean by the love of God—namely, that despite the commonsensical imperfection of things, they were nonetheless loved by God just as they are, and that this loving of them was at the same time the godding of them. This time the vivid sensation of lightness and clarity lasted a full week."[30]

When Watts adds that "these experiences, reinforced by others that have followed, have been the enlivening force of all my work in writing and in philosophy since that time,"[31] one understands why a concern with mysticism characterizes his numerous books, which have made his name known in England and Europe as well as in America. Though he has written of both Eastern and Western mysticism, the interest in the East that he revealed in his first book— *The Spirit of Zen* (1936), a popularization of Suzuki's works—has never waned. In *Behold the Spirit* (1947), his main argument was for a revival of Christianity through renewed emphasis upon the mystical meaning of the Incarnation, yet he also advocated the spiritual wisdom of Zen, remarking that "the metaphysical background of Zen is the philosophy of Mahayana Buddhism," and that "there can be no doubt whatever that this kind of Buddhist *mysticism* is as genuine an experience of God as that ineffable mystery known in Christian mysticism as the 'Cloud of Unknowing' or the 'luminous darkness.' " In *The Supreme Identity*, published in 1950, the year that he left the Episcopal Church, he pointed out similarities in the mysticism of East and West, and placed his emphasis upon the Eastern doctrines, especially Vedanta, declaring "the true end of man" to be "the realization of the Supreme Identity of *atma* and *Brahma*, of the Self and the infinite." During the fifties and sixties he continued to advocate the Eastern teachings. In *Beyond Theology* (1964) he argued that the best way to understand Christianity was to examine it "in the context of the world-view of the Hindus."[32]

While maintaining his interest in Oriental mysticism, he changed his interpretation of mystical experience. In *Behold the Spirit* and *The Supreme Identity* he had interpreted it in the traditional manner as supernatural experience, but after 1950 he modified his views so that they accorded with modern scientific theories of man and the universe, such as relativity and field theory. By 1960 he was writing of the mystic: "His sphere of experience is the unspeakable. Yet this need mean no more than that it is the sphere of physical nature, of all that is not simply conceptions, numbers, or words." Putting it another way, he suggested that mystical experience "might best be described as insight, as the word is now used in psychiatry." He was "more and more persuaded," he said in 1961, that "so-called mystical consciousness" is not "supernatural or metaphysical in the usual sense."[33]

His changed view of mystical experience was evident in his main work on Zen Buddhism, *The Way of Zen*, which appeared in 1957. His comment on satori, for instance, seemed designed to bring Suzuki down to earth. It should not be assumed, he wrote,

that *satori* is a single, sudden leap from the common consciousness to "complete, unexcelled awakening". . . . *Satori* really designates the sudden and intuitive way of seeing into anything, whether it be remembering a forgotten name or seeing into the deepest principles of Buddhism. One seeks and seeks, but cannot find. One then gives up, and the answer comes by itself. Thus there may be many occasions of *satori* in the course of training, great *satori* and little *satori*, and the solution of many of the *koan* depends upon nothing more sensational than a kind of "knack" for understanding the Zen style of handling Buddhist principles.

He did not claim personal experience of satori. Neither did he represent himself "as a Zenist, or even as a Buddhist." Rather, he preferred to take a "friendly neutral position" toward institutionalized Zen—that is, the kind with which Suzuki and other Japanese and American Zenists were associated. His *Way* emphasized the Taoist origins of Zen, and repeatedly he called attention to its humanistic aspects, which derive from its identification of Nirvana with the phenomenal world. "The perfection of Zen," he declared, "is to be perfectly and simply human. The difference of the adept in Zen from the ordinary run of men is that the latter are, in one way or another, at odds with their own humanity, and are attempting to be angels or demons."[34] Though he did not neglect such mystical Zen teachings as timelessness and the unreality of the ego, on the whole his way seems considerably more mundane than Suzuki's.

Yet in Suzuki's writings as well as in Watts's, readers could find a way so complex and enigmatic that it might easily appeal both to those who sought salvation in heaven and those who sought it on earth. And in the America of the fifties there were many seekers. War and the threat of war, and the atomic bomb with its potentiality for destroying the human race, had spurred intensified questioning of Western man's model of the universe, based upon faith in science and technology. What was the individual's relation to this mysterious, dangerous universe? Intellectuals asked the old question anew, and some sought answers in the religious existentialism of Søren Kierkegaard, or in Sartre's atheistic anguish, while others found solace in orthodox Christianity. Still others, as we have seen, turned to Vedanta, and increasing numbers were drawn to Zen Buddhism —not, for the most part, as devotees, yet often as serious inquirers.

Zen was likely to be especially attractive to those who as members of the American armed forces had encountered it in Korea or Japan, perhaps gaining some firsthand knowledge of how deeply this one minority sect of Buddhism has influenced not only religion and philosophy but also art, literature, architecture, and other facets of culture in that part of the world. In addition, it could appeal to the Western mind, long accustomed to Freudian introspection, as a kind of Oriental psychotherapy. C. G. Jung and Erich Fromm, among others, compared it with psychotherapy in the West.[35] Their interest in Zen helped to bring it to the attention of the general public.

Popular interest in Zen reached a peak in America during the late fifties. Watts, like Suzuki, both wrote and lectured, and he did not neglect the audiences of radio and television. In popular magazines, articles on Watts and Suzuki and Zen Buddhism multiplied. In academic quarterlies, scholars compared Zen thought with Western philosophy and Zen art with Western painting. In music, the composer John Cage drew inspiration, so he said, from Zenist silence. And in the bohemian districts of the nation's cities, from New York to San Francisco, unconventional young people known as the "Beat Generation" or "Beats" mixed Zen with poetry, painting, free love, alcohol, and marijuana. Their chief spokesman, Jack Kerouac, used Zen ideas in his widely read novel, *The Dharma Bums* (1958).

Both Watts and Suzuki expressed doubt that what the Beats practiced was really Zen. Watts published a provocative essay, "Beat Zen, Square Zen, and Zen," in which he criticized not only the "Bohemian affectations" of the Beats but also the traditional Zen of Japan, which he regarded as overly formal and fussy— in a word, "square." As he had previously indicated in his *Way of Zen,* he preferred the life-style of "the old Chinese Zen masters," who were "steeped in Taoism," and whose "Zen was *wu-shih,* which means approximately 'nothing special' or 'no fuss.' " Suzuki suggested that the Zen from which the Beat artists professed to draw inspiration was not authentic. To Kerouac's proclamation that the Beat poets were "CHILDREN . . . childlike graybeard Homers singing in the street," he replied, "Yes, there is enough of childishness but not much of childlikeness. Spontaneity is not everything, it must be 'rooted.' " In his opinion, the Beats needed to develop "the primary feeling for the

Self."[36] Apparently they never did, and soon their enthusiasm for Zen faded from public view along with the short-lived Beat movement.

Meanwhile a fresh current of traditional Zen mysticism was entering American thought. Native Americans who had received Zen training in Japan were beginning to speak out. The first voice was that of Ruth Fuller Sasaki, widow of Sokei-an Sasaki, who, it will be remembered, had founded the First Zen Institute of America. Long interested in Buddhist enlightenment, she had visited Japan in the early thirties and studied Zen in a Kyoto monastery; later in New York she had been a disciple of Sokei-an, whom she married in 1944. After his death she resumed her studies in Kyoto, where in the late fifties she established a branch of the First Zen Institute as a center for American Zenists studying in Japan. The center became a subtemple of Daitoku-ji Monastery, and in May 1958, at the age of sixty-five, Ruth Sasaki was ordained its priest, thus becoming, in the words of *Time* magazine, "the first American in history to be admitted to the Japanese Buddhist priesthood and installed as head priest of a Japanese temple."[37] That same year she published a brief monograph, *Zen: A Religion*, following it with *Zen: A Method for Religious Awakening* (1959), an address which she had delivered in the fall of 1958 at the Massachusetts Institute of Technology. In 1966, as co-author with the Zen master Miura Isshu, she published an authoritative book, *Zen Dust: The History of the Koan and Koan Study in Rinzai (Lin-Chi) Zen.* It contained her history of the koan and her translation of lectures in Japanese that Miura Isshu had given in New York in 1955 at the First Zen Institute.

In these writings Ruth Sasaki stresses the religious, the mystical, and the moral nature of Zen Buddhism. Zazen practice, in her view, is fundamental, and "morality is the foundation stone of practice; without morality there can be no true practice and therefore no true attainment." Right living, zazen, and koan study lead to satori, the experience of the undifferentiated realm of the mystic, in which "God—if I may borrow that word for a moment—the universe, and man are one indissoluble existence, one total whole."[38]

This traditional view of Zen found another voice in America when in 1964 Paul Wienpahl published *The Matter of Zen: A Brief Account of Zazen.* Wienpahl, a professor of philosophy at the University of California, Santa Barbara, who had studied Zen in Kyoto under Ruth Sasaki's direction, dwelt at length upon the importance of zazen, and indicated that he himself had attained at least some degree of the egoless, unitive experience in which "the moral precept to 'love thy neighbor as thyself' suddenly appears . . . as a description of fact and no longer as a command." "Plato was right," he concluded. "There is knowledge of the Good."[39]

The most eloquent advocate of traditional Japanese Zen, Philip Kapleau, is a former American businessman who in 1965 became a Zen priest. His book *The Three Pillars of Zen: Teaching, Practice, and Enlightenment,* published in Tokyo in 1965 and in New York in 1966, is an extraordinary compilation of lectures by his Zen teacher, Yasutani-roshi, of interviews between the master and his students, and of autobiographical narratives in which Japanese and American Zenists describe their enlightenment experiences. Kapleau makes necessary translations from the Japanese, and binds the whole together with editorial introductions that add up to a trenchant commentary on Zen Buddhism. One of the enlightenment narratives is his. Told in extracts from his diary, it is a revealing story of spiritual quest and transformation.

In 1953 Kapleau, a forty-year-old bachelor, was prospering in the court reporting business and finding life meaningless. Regularly he commuted from his home in New Haven, Connecticut, to New York City to attend the Columbia University lectures of Suzuki, whom he had met briefly in Japan during the American occupation, while serving as court reporter with the International Military Tribunal at Tokyo. Suzuki's expositions of Zen

115

philosophy intrigued but puzzled him, affording no relief from his personal problems. He suffered from allergies and stomach ulcers, and could not sleep without drugs. "So miserable wish I had the guts to end it all," he wrote in his diary.[40]

Instead of committing suicide he quit his business, went back to Japan, and plunged into five arduous years of Zen practice under the guidance of three successive *roshis,* or spiritual teachers, the last being Yasutani-roshi. Frustrations piled on top of disappointments, but he persisted in his quest, and there came a sesshin in August, 1958, when Yasutani-roshi warned him to hold fast to his zazen and his koan, for he was near Self-realization. Through the night of August 4 and on into the next day he practiced, losing all sense of self, absorbed in meditation even while eating or sweeping floors. In his diary he recorded what happened that afternoon when he had his formal interview with Zen master Yasutani.

> Hawklike, the roshi scrutinized me as I entered his room, walked toward him, prostrated myself, and sat before him with my mind alert and exhilarated. . . .
>
> "The universe is One," he began, each word tearing into my mind like a bullet. "The moon of Truth—" All at once the roshi, the room, every single thing disappeared in a dazzling stream of illumination and I felt myself bathed in a delicious, unspeakable delight. . . . For a fleeting eternity I was alone—I alone was. . . . Then the roshi swam into view. Our eyes met and flowed into each other, and we burst out laughing. . . .
>
> "I have it! I know! There is nothing, absolutely nothing. I am everything and everything is nothing!" I exclaimed more to myself than to the roshi, and got up and walked out. . . .

At the evening interview Yasutani-roshi questioned him on his koan and confirmed his kensho. "Although your realization is clear," he explained, "you can expand and deepen it infinitely. . . ." Kapleau resumed his zazen.

On August 9 he noted the after-effects of his experience: "Feel free as a fish swimming in an ocean of cool, clear water after being stuck in a tank of glue. . . . and so grateful for everything. . . . grateful to everyone who encouraged and sustained me

116

in spite of my immature personality and stubborn nature.

"But mostly I am grateful for my human body, for the privilege as a human being to know this Joy, like no other."[41]

Kapleau's Buddhist interpretation of enlightenment accords with that of Suzuki and Ruth Sasaki. With enlightenment, he writes, comes "the realization that the substratum of existence is a Voidness out of which all things ceaselessly arise and into which they endlessly return, that this Emptiness is positive and alive and in fact not other than the vividness of a sunset or the harmonies of a great symphony.

"This bursting into consciousness of the effulgent Buddha-nature is the 'swallowing up' of the universe, the obliteration of every feeling of opposition and separateness. In this state of unconditioned subjectivity I, *selfless* I, am supreme."

His main concern, however, is not philosophy but practice. He stresses the moral, religious nature of Zen and its inseparability from zazen, which may be practiced as sitting (the chief form), walking, chanting, or manual labor. "At its profoundest level Zen, like every other great religion, transcends its own teachings and practices," he concedes, "yet at the same time there is no Zen apart from these practices. The attempt in the West to isolate Zen in a vacuum of the intellect, cut off from the very disciplines which are its *raison d'être*, has nourished a pseudo-Zen which is little more than a mind-tickling diversion of highbrows and a plaything of beatniks."[42]

Wishing to correct such "distortion," he takes issue with other writers who, in his opinion, have obscured true Zen. Suzuki seems to be one target of the remark that "certain exponents of Zen, Asians as well as Westerners, have misled their readers" by overly indulging their "relish for drama" and giving disproportionate space to "the beatings and kickings of the ancient Chinese masters," together with their paradoxical outbursts, such as, " 'You must kill the Buddha!' " Watts is criticized as being too theoretical, and for questioning, in his *Way of Zen*, the importance of sitting in zazen. As for the "beatnik," his actions reveal his lack of enlightenment. "The freedom of the liberated Zen man is a far cry from the 'freedom' of the Zen beatnik, driven as the latter is by his uncontrolled selfish desires. The inseparable bond with his fellow men which the truly enlightened feels precludes any such self-centered behavior as the beatnik's."[43]

In making these criticisms, Kapleau does not mean to present himself as an exceptional American, happily escaped from a land fit only for pseudo Zen. On the contrary, he sees affinity between the Zen way and the American spirit. "In Zen's emphasis on self-reliance, in its clear awareness of the dangers of intellectualism, in its empirical appeal to personal experience and not philosophic speculation as the means of verifying ultimate truth, in its pragmatic concern with mind and suffering, and in its direct, practical methods for body-mind emancipation, Americans find much that is congenial to their native temperament, their historical conditioning, and their particular *Weltanschauung.*"

Of course Zen is not merely for Japanese and Americans, but for all. It offers salvation to everyone in this modern age of anxiety. As Kapleau, with the optimism of the mystic, puts it: ". . . the fact that ordinary people through satori can discover meaning and joy in life, as well as a sense of their own uniqueness and solidarity with all mankind, surely spells hope for men everywhere."[44]

That men everywhere, and in America in particular, have not yet in large numbers found Zen to be their most congenial way of salvation is obvious. By the time Kapleau's book appeared, the American vogue for Zen was over. Yet serious Zenists in the United States, guided by visiting or immigrant Japanese teachers, continued to practice the traditional disciplines and occasionally to establish new centers. Kapleau returned, after thirteen years in Japan, and in 1966 founded and became spiritual director of the Zen Meditation Center of Rochester, New York, where he sought to Americanize traditional rituals. In 1967, the Zen Center of San Francisco established its Zen Mountain Center, including a Soto monastery for both men and women, at Tassajara in central California. By 1969 a number of active centers could be found in the United States, not only in New York

City, Rochester, San Francisco, and Los Angeles, but also in Philadelphia, Washington, Cambridge, and Honolulu.[45] As the decade ended, it seemed evident that the mysticism first brought by Soyen Shaku and Suzuki had entered permanently into American thought and, through the quietly growing Zen movement, into American practice.

CHAPTER 7

Psychology and Psychedelic Experience

In this chapter the psychological approach to mysticism that we have touched on intermittently from William James to Suzuki becomes our main theme. Three aspects of this approach concern us: the expression of mysticism within the psychological frame of thought, the continuing interest of psychologists in mystical experience, and the upsurge in the fifties and sixties of psychedelic experimentation inspired by a dramatic revival of the argument that chemical agents can induce mystical states of consciousness.

We have noticed that Western mystics like Rufus Jones have occasionally taken sharp issue with the psychological approach —witness Jones' debate with James Leuba over the validity of mystical experience and the competence of psychologists to judge it. Neither have the Oriental mystics who have spoken to America been much at ease with Western psychology. Rather they hold to Eastern traditions that blend the mystical with the psychological. Vedantic mysticism, as we have seen, embraces Patanjali's system of yoga, which has been called "one of the great psychological achievements of all time."[1] This system, Swami Prabhavananda points out, "deals specifically with the process of mind control," and accepts not only "the subconscious mind" but also "the superconscious state." The harmony of Indian psychology and mysticism is a recurrent theme of

Prabhavananda's *Spiritual Heritage of India.* [2]

Swami Akhilananda—author, it will be remembered, of the *Hindu View of Christ*—has published two books expressing mystical thought as psychology. His *Hindu Psychology: Its Meaning for the West* was introduced to American readers in 1946 by Gordon W. Allport of the Harvard psychology department and Edgar Sheffield Brightman of the philosophy department of Boston University. It mingles learned discussion of Western and Hindu psychological theory with unreserved acceptance of the mystical "superconscious state." Akhilananda takes issue with Jung for identifying superconscious experiences with the "deep unconscious state," describing them as "vast but dim," and declaring that they are "scarcely to be recommended anywhere north of the Tropic of Cancer." Jung's comment is "unscientific," he argues. "Any man who has had these realizations will laugh at such conclusions." The superconscious state, samadhi, is not dim, but "vivid and definite." North of the Tropic of Cancer it has been recommended by "Judaeo-Christian types" like St. Teresa and Meister Eckhart who, unlike Jung, speak from experience. And far from its being identical with the unconscious state, it is, in its profound awareness, the very opposite. "To identify the superconscious state with the unconscious state is to mix darkness and light. In one case man is completely oblivious of the existence of God; in the other case man is fully aware of the existence of God, nay, identified with Him." [3]

Mysticism also permeates Akhilananda's *Mental Health and Hindu Psychology* (1951). In this study he declares that Hindu psychology grew out of spiritual experience, and is closely related to the mental health field, since the Hindus "fully realize that until and unless the mind is wholly unified and integrated there is no possibility of spiritual realization or mystical experiences." [4] He goes on to argue that the fears and anxieties, the conflicts and frustrations that make for mental illness can be overcome by yogic meditation and mystical attainment. Meditation strengthens the will, stabilizes the emotions, and calms the mind, and when mystical experience results it is even more conducive to mental health. The man who truly realizes his oneness with God lives free of negative tensions—in peace and love.

Like Akhilananda, Suzuki has been well aware of the psychological implications of his mystical way, and has called attention to them. He writes of "the psychological aspect of satori" and, as we noted, follows William James in setting forth distinguishing marks of this mystical state. Perhaps James also influenced Suzuki's suggestion, in his first series of *Essays*, that "the power to see into the nature of one's own being" may lie hidden in "an unknown region in our consciousness" that is "sometimes called the Unconscious or the Subconscious."[5] This sounds like the *Varieties*. But Suzuki elsewhere gives a different meaning to "the Unconscious." In his third series of *Essays* and again in *The Zen Doctrine of No-Mind* (1949), he applies the term to the mystical state which the Chinese Zen Master Hui-neng designated by the terms *Wu-nien* or *Wu-hsin*, meaning literally "no-thought" or "no-mind," and connoting "no-consciousness." For the broad Chinese meaning, explains Suzuki, "it is difficult to find an English equivalent except the Unconscious, though even this must be used in a definitely limited sense. It is not the Unconscious in its usual psychological sense, nor in the sense given it by the analytical psychologists, who find it very much deeper than mere lack of consciousness, but probably in the sense of the 'abysmal ground' of the mediaeval mystics, or in the sense of the Divine Will even before its utterance of the Word."[6]

It seems, then, that Suzuki, like Rufus Jones, was initially intrigued by James' treatment of the unconscious in the *Varieties*, but eventually moved away from that theory to more thoroughly mystical ground. In view of his shifting position, and his occasional ambiguity as to whether he is referring to the Freudian or the mystical unconscious, it is not surprising that psychotherapists have found their own theories in his writings. When in 1949 Jung wrote the Foreword to a new edition of Suzuki's *Introduction to Zen Buddhism*, he suggested that satori was "the final break-through of unconscious contents into the

the conscious,"[7] and that in this regard Zen had much in common with psychotherapy. When in 1960 Erich Fromm collaborated with Suzuki in the publication of *Zen Buddhism and Psychoanalysis,* Fromm attempted to show similarities between Zen and psychoanalysis, arguing that both aim at "the transformation of unconsciousness into consciousness."[8]

Fromm's argument turns upon Suzuki's discussion, in the same book, of the Zen effort "to become . . . conscious of the unconscious,"[9] and evidently the psychoanalyst assumes that the Zenist is using "the unconscious" in the Freudian sense. Actually Suzuki seems to be using it in the mystical sense. For in his lectures on Zen which comprise the first portion of the book—lectures which he delivered in 1957 to a conference of some fifty psychiatrists and psychologists, including Fromm—he states, "What I mean by 'the unconscious' and what psychoanalysts mean by it may be different. . . ." What he means by it, he goes on to say, might be termed "metascientific," or "antescientific," or even "antiscientific." He couples it with "no-mind," and likens it to St. Augustine's selfless love of God. Perhaps, he suggests, "this kind of unconscious" might be called "the Cosmic Unconscious."[10] These and other similar remarks sprinkled through his discourse indicate that he is not discussing Zen as a form of Oriental psychoanalysis, but as mysticism.

If Suzuki has not completely subscribed to the basic tenets of depth psychology, neither has the well-known sociologist, Pitirim A. Sorokin. Although Sorokin is a scientist-philosopher with religious faith rather than a mystic,[11] he has been markedly sympathetic toward mysticism, and as director of the Harvard Research Center in Creative Altruism has conducted studies of unselfish love that have involved the investigation of mysticism from the standpoint of psychology. On the basis of these studies he declared in 1954 that "the 'depth psychology' of the prevalent theories of personality is in fact quite shallow. It either flattens the mental structure almost exclusively to the level of the unconscious or subconscious, with a sort of epiphenomenal and vague 'ego' and 'superego,' or just depicts it as a 'two-story building'—

123

the unconscious (subconscious) and the conscious (rational)."
He suggested that the structure be viewed as fourfold. "Four
different forms of energies—four mental levels and activities—
can be distinguished in our total personality and behavior: 1) the
biologically unconscious (subconscious); 2) the biologically conscious; 3) the socioculturally conscious; and 4) the supraconscious."

"The supraconscious," he explains, "is egoless: it transcends
ego entirely and unconditionally." It is a mystical state of consciousness, such as the "divine madness" of Plato, the satori of
Zen Buddhism, or the samadhi of the yogi. Its importance can
hardly be exaggerated, for it "seems to be the fountainhead of
the greatest achievements and discoveries in all fields of human
creative activity: science, religion, philosophy, technology, ethics, law, the fine arts, economics, and politics."[12]

In an effort to demonstrate the reality of the supraconscious,
Thérèse Brosse, writer on yoga and sometime head of the cardio-
logical clinic of the Faculty of Medicine of Paris University,
went to India under the auspices of Sorokin's Research Center
and made electrocardiograms and other instrumental recordings
of the effects of yogic exercises designed to produce samadhi. As
her subjects moved from ordinary consciousness into what they
reported as the mystical state, her instruments recorded variations in the subjects' respiration and heart action. What these
variations revealed about yoga she hesitated to say; she concluded that her study was "fragmentary" and that "much research will be necessary to lift even a corner of the veil." Sorokin
less cautiously decided that Dr. Brosse's "pioneer study instru-
mentally confirmed the tangible effects of the supraconscious
upon the activities of heart, lungs, and other organs. . . ."[13]

In the fifties, as Sorokin published these theories and investi-
gations of the mystical consciousness and sought to broaden the
organizational base of his many-sided research into creative
altruism, he won the approval of scholarly mystics as well as
nonmystical scholars. Akhilananda contributed to one of the
Research Center volumes an essay on the Vedantist way to

mental health.[14] He also joined Sorokin and others in organizing, in 1955, the Research Society in Creative Altruism. The Society then convened, at the Massachusetts Institute of Technology, a Conference on New Knowledge in Human Values attended by "several hundred scientists and scholars," including Suzuki. But the Society did not last. "Mainly because of lack of necessary funds," explained Sorokin, it could not realize its plans "and, after a few years of quiet existence, died."[15] The Research Center also declined for lack of funds, after publishing some eleven volumes written or edited by Sorokin. On retiring as professor emeritus in 1959 he transferred it from Harvard to the American Academy of Arts and Sciences and reduced its research to his own studies.

For a time, then, Sorokin threw his special scientific spotlight upon the mystical consciousness. But the psychological approach to mysticism that stirred up the greatest amount of public excitement in the fifties and sixties was not his; neither was it anything sanctioned by Zen or Vedanta. Beyond doubt it was psychedelic experimentation—more technically advanced than, yet similar to, the earlier chemical ventures of Benjamin Blood and William James.

Aldous Huxley heralded the new psychedelic enthusiasm when in 1954 he published *The Doors of Perception*. Taking his title from William Blake's declaration, "If the doors of perception were cleansed every thing would appear to man as it is, infinite," he first sketched for his readers the latest scientific research on psychedelic drugs, including mescaline and LSD (lysergic acid diethylamide), and then told how "one bright May morning" in 1953 in his Hollywood home he "swallowed four-tenths of a gram of mescalin dissolved in half a glass of water and sat down to wait for the results." When they came they seemed fraught with mystical significance. His "I" became "Not-self," as he expressed it, and it appeared to him that ordinary objects around him such as the furniture, the flowers in a vase, and the books on his study shelves were glowing with jewel-like colors and manifesting an inner meaning that he compared to the "Is-

125

ness" of Meister Eckhart's philosophy and the Suchness of Zen Buddhism. This, he decided, was "contemplation at its height. At its height, but not yet in its fullness." The fullness was lacking because mescaline "gives access to . . . a contemplation that is incompatible with action and even with the will to action, the very thought of action. In the intervals between his revelations the mescalin taker is apt to feel that, though in one way everything is supremely as it should be, in another there is something wrong. His problem is essentially the same as that which confronts the quietist. . . ." However, every form of contemplation, "even the most quietistic," has "its ethical values," and contemplatives are not likely to engage in evil activities.

Together with this favorable view of his first psychedelic experience Huxley set forth a few reservations. He pointed out that mescaline is not "the ideal drug," since its effects last inconveniently long and it can plunge "a minority" of takers into hell instead of heaven. He also declared, "I am not so foolish as to equate what happens under the influence of mescalin or of any other drug, prepared or in the future preparable, with the realization of the end and ultimate purpose of human life: Enlightenment, the Beatific Vision. All I am suggesting is that the mescalin experience is what Catholic theologians call 'a gratuitous grace,' not necessary to salvation but potentially helpful and to be accepted thankfully, if made available." Still he went on to suggest that overly rational, overly verbal intellectuals ought to be "urged and even, if necessary, compelled to take an occasional trip through some chemical Door in the Wall into the world of transcendental experience."

As for "the aspiring mystic," Huxley advised him in a sequel essay, *Heaven and Hell* (1956) to shun old-fashioned methods like fasting, to learn "the chemical conditions of transcendental experience," and to "turn for technical help to the specialists— in pharmacology, in biochemistry, in physiology and neurology, in psychology and psychiatry, and parapsychology." The chemical method that he advocated was the ingestion of "either mescalin or lysergic acid." These two drugs he equated with hypnosis as means of altering consciousness that "are sufficiently reliable, sufficiently easy and sufficiently safe to justify their employment by those who know what they are doing."[16]

In 1958, writing for the *Saturday Evening Post*, he again emphasized the mystical significance of mescaline and LSD. "It lowers the barrier between conscious and subconscious," he wrote of LSD, "and permits the patient to look more deeply and understandingly into the recesses of his own mind. The deepening of self-knowledge takes place against a background of visionary and even mystical experience." Again, he declared that "a person who takes LSD or mescaline may suddenly understand —not only intellectually but organically, experientially—the meaning of such tremendous religious affirmations as 'God is love,' or 'Though He slay me, yet will I trust in Him.'" He looked forward to a near future when this kind of "temporary self-transcendence," which "is no guarantee of permanent enlightenment," would become widely available through low-cost drugs. Then, "instead of being rare, premystical and mystical experiences will become common."[17]

Quite obviously his advocacy of these powerful drugs was not cautious. It should be remembered that he wrote before the emergence into print of much that is now known about their negative effects. Could he have read, for example, the medical warnings in Dr. Sidney Cohen's *The Beyond Within: The LSD Story* (1964), or in Dr. Donald B. Louria's *The Drug Scene* (1968), he doubtless would have tempered his enthusiasm.

His optimistic view of the drugs was of course shaped by his continuing experience with them. This seems to have been wholly satisfactory. Gerald Heard states that after using mescaline Huxley found that LSD "served him even better," and that his long study and practice of meditation enabled him to employ the drug effectively. "For him, then, LSD was a sacrament, a perfect psycho-physical aid to sustain the mind at its utmost reach."[18]

A sacrament—this the psychedelic experience clearly is in Huxley's last novel, *Island* (1962), which describes a Utopia named Pala. In Pala the religion is a Huxleyan distillation of Mahayana Buddhism, and the children are initiated into adolescence by a mountain-climbing ordeal followed by a temple rite in which they attain mystical experience by taking a psychedelic drug made from mushrooms. In the end Will Farnaby, the cynical British journalist who accidentally discovers Pala, also takes the drug and has experiences paralleling those described by Huxley in *The Doors of Perception.* So convinced is he of the existence of God and the rightness of the universe that he remains serene, contemplating a flowering hibiscus transformed into a burning bush, while a neighboring dictator seizes Pala in a midnight coup d'état.[19] Reading this, one cannot help thinking what Huxley evidently does not intend to imply, that Farnaby's attitude toward the murder and subjugation of his friends is extremely quietistic.

Actually, the mystical philosophy that Huxley explicitly advocates in *Island* is the opposite of quietism. Its heart, as one of the islanders explains to Farnaby, is *"tat tvam asi,* 'thou art That' "; but the realization of this truth, by means of the mushroom drug and various forms of yoga, does not justify trying "to escape into a Nirvana apart from life." Here the novelist expresses a growing belief of his later years, the conviction that the Bodhisattva ideal of service in the world is best and that there ought to be, in the words of his wife Laura Archera Huxley, "no dropping out from Love and Work, even from an unsatisfactory society, into the personal isolated security of Pure Light with or without psychedelics."[20]

As mysticism sanctifies daily life in Pala, so does it illuminate the act of dying. Farnaby witnesses the death of an elderly woman stricken with cancer. Her husband sits beside her bed, speaking lovingly to her and helping her to pass peacefully into the Light, in the manner described in the Tibetan Book of the Dead. The scene is drawn from Huxley's personal experience. In 1955, when his first wife, Maria, died of cancer, he bent over her and continuously whispered to her words of peace and love. In an account of her death written for a few friends, he told how he helped her to visualize "the One Reality" as light by reminding her of the light that had been associated with "a number of genuinely mystical experiences" that had come to her in previous years while they were living in the Mojave Desert. Because of these experiences, he felt, she "had lived with an abiding sense of divine immanence, of Reality totally present, moment by moment in every object, person and event." And so they shared the same mystical goal as he whispered, "Peace, love, joy *now*. Being *now*. . . . Let go, let go. Forget the body, leave it lying here; it is of no importance now. Go forward into the light." When finally "the breathing ceased," he wrote, "it was without any struggle."[21]

Thus fact inspired the fiction of *Island*. Nor was this all. In November 1963, in his Hollywood residence, Huxley himself lay dying of neck cancer with his second wife, Laura, at his bedside. He had been reluctant to admit, openly, that his severe illness might prove fatal, and several times in the two previous months had declined LSD that Laura had offered him, saying that he would wait until his health improved. On the morning of November 22 he scrawled a note to her on his writing tablet: "LSD—Try it 100 mm intramuscular." She went to another room to get the drug, saw the doctor, the nurse, and other members of the household gathered around the television set, and learned that President John F. Kennedy had been assassinated. Tragedy —but there was no time to think about it. Declining the doctor's offer of assistance, she returned and administered the LSD herself, following it an hour later with a second injection after Huxley had indicated his willingness to accept it. She knew that with the aid of the drug that he regarded as a sacrament he was preparing for death, and she began to speak to him of going into the light, as he had once spoken to Maria.

Hours passed. Now and then her emotion would overcome her and she would quickly leave the bedside, returning when she was able to speak calmly. Once she asked him, "Do you hear me?" and he squeezed her hand. Death came at 5:20 P.M. with a gradual slowing, a gentle cessation, of breath. Aldous Huxley died peacefully, listening to "forward . . . into the light."

When in 1968 Laura Huxley revealed these intimate details in her memoir of her husband's last years, *This Timeless Moment*, she expressed concern over what she regarded as "the public abuse" of psychedelic drugs. "In the years between 1953 and 1963," she wrote, "Aldous had about ten or twelve chemically induced psychedelic experiences: *the total amount of chemical taken during those ten years was not as much as many people take today in a single week, sometimes in a single dose.*"[22]

The note of alarm in this statement was frequently sounded by knowledgeable persons in the late sixties, when ominous clouds had gathered in the psychedelic sky. At first, however, optimism prevailed, and popular and scholarly periodicals rivaled the Sunday supplements in publishing generally favorable articles on the "magic mushroom" from which psilocybin is derived; on the ritual use of peyote (the natural source of mescaline) among North American Indian tribes; and on the mystical and psychotherapeutic implications of the powerful synthetic, LSD. In the scientific literature, these and similar consciousness-changing agents were usually referred to as "psychotomimetic" drugs, meaning that they mimicked psychosis; but in the popular accounts they were more often called "hallucinogens" (producers of hallucinations) or "psychedelic" (mind-manifesting) drugs, the latter word having been coined by Humphry Osmond (Aldous Huxley's mentor) because he considered the other terms inaccurate. As radio and television joined the other mass media in stimulating public interest, a boom in psychedelic drug-taking developed, overlapping the Zen boom of the late fifties and continuing with growing momentum in the early sixties.

Prominent among those who followed Huxley as advocates of psychedelic experience was Timothy Leary, lecturer on clinical psychology at Harvard. In August 1960, while vacationing in Mexico, Leary ate seven psychedelic mushrooms and had what he later described as an experience of deep religious significance. On returning to Harvard he began experimenting with psilocybin on himself, his friends, and various volunteers, eventually using LSD instead of the mushroom drug. A Harvard colleague, Richard Alpert, became his partner in research. Aldous Huxley, who happened to be spending the fall of 1960 in Cambridge, helped plan the first experiments, and as the research progressed many another well-known figure found his way to Leary's door. The Beat poet Allen Ginsberg came to visit and have his psychedelic experience; so also did Gerald Heard and Alan Watts.[23]

By 1963 Leary's unconventional ways had produced sensational publicity in the press, and he and Alpert were dismissed from Harvard, after which they began careers as proselytizers for a revolutionary, religious way of life involving the use of psychedelic drugs as sacraments. In 1964, with Ralph Metzner and Alpert, Leary published *The Psychedelic Experience: A Manual Based on the Tibetan Book of the Dead.* In 1968 he brought out two more books, *The Politics of Ecstasy,* a compilation of his articles, speeches, and interviews, and *High Priest,* an autobiographical account of his initial psychedelic adventures. In these flamboyant writings he argued for psychedelic experience in eclectic scientific and religious terms, including references to Vedantist and Zenist mysticism. As author, lecturer, and defendant in the courts against various charges of violating the drug laws, he became the most influential and controversial figure of the psychedelic boom.

This spreading usage of consciousness-changing drugs was an unprecedented social phenomenon in America. It could be partly explained by the appeal of Oriental mysticism, linked with psychedelic experience by Huxley, Watts, Leary, and other authors, including popular songsters. It could be further explained by the massive publicity that, in an era of instant communication and accelerating social change, drummed incessantly upon the exciting new wonders of LSD and the activities and arguments of its more colorful advocates. Leary, for instance, drew much attention in 1966 when he declared in an interview in *Playboy* magazine, "There is no question that LSD is the most powerful aphrodisiac ever discovered by man," a statement promptly challenged by Dr. Louria and others as being contrary to fact.[24]

131

Social analysts seeking additional causes of the boom pointed out that it was chiefly—though of course not entirely—a young people's movement, that about half of the nation's population was under the age of twenty-five, and that the college population, which seemed especially interested in psychedelics, numbered nearly six million. They suggested that many of these young people felt socially alienated, for a variety of reasons: the war in Vietnam, the impact of racial prejudice, conflict with parents, discontent with the affluent society, despair over life in its slums—the list ran the gamut of America's social problems. Neither did the analysts overlook the appeal of psychedelics to the mentally unstable, the examples in alcoholism and lawlessness set the young by their elders, or the affinity between introspective psychedelic devotees and introspective radicals of the New Left.[25] Indeed it seemed possible to adduce an almost endless series of interrelated factors, depending upon how thoroughly one wished to pursue the analysis.

As to the number of young people actually using psychedelics, estimates varied widely. Dr. Louria, long associated with Bellevue Hospital and president of the New York State Council on Drug Addiction, suggested: "... a reasonable guess for 1966–1967 would be that, countrywide, in the range of .5 per cent to 2 per cent of college students had used LSD or a similar potent hallucinogen such as dimethyltryptamine (DMT), psilocybin or mescaline." Marijuana usage among college students he estimated at 15 per cent, and he noted that most marijuana users merely experimented with it a few times and quit. But its use was spreading in the nation's high schools and in the Armed Forces.[26]

Conspicuous among devotees of psychedelic drugs were the "Hippies," young bohemians who in the mid-sixties gravitated to low-rent metropolitan areas like the Haight-Ashbury district of San Francisco and the East Village of New York. More joyous than their Beat predecessors, they proclaimed a philosophy of communal living, peace, love, and religious seeking. Picturesquely dressed, with beads and bells and flowers in their long hair, they danced in the streets, were photographed by the news media, and drew great numbers of other "flower children," many of them runaways from middle-class homes, to join them. "Summer 1967," *Newsweek* reported, "brought an influx of about 50,000 young people" to Haight-Ashbury.[27] With this mass pilgrimage the psychedelic boom seemed to reach its peak of optimism.

To be sure, critical voices had long since been raised against the new enthusiasm, and among intellectuals interested in psychedelics and mysticism sharp debate had arisen over this key question: Could chemical agents, particularly psychedelic drugs, induce genuine mystical experience? If the answer was Yes, then seekers had good reason to use psychedelics, and traditional views of mysticism would have to be revised to take account of chemically induced ecstasy. If the answer was No, then the traditional views would stand unchanged, and mysticism should not be invoked to justify drug-taking.

A resounding No was registered in 1957 when R. C. Zaehner, professor of Eastern religions and ethics at Oxford, took issue in his *Mysticism Sacred and Profane* with the mystical claims for mescaline that Huxley had advanced in *The Doors of Perception.* Arguing from an avowed Roman Catholic standpoint, Zaehner branded as "absurd arrogance" Huxley's belief that his mescaline experience was "contemplation at its height," and contended that the novelist's drug-heightened perception of form and color was nothing more than "the natural mystical experience," which had no connection with "the direct experience of God in his unutterable holiness."[28] Zaehner had experimentally tested Huxley's hypothesis by taking mescaline himself; he reported that the experience was trivial.

His argument won the approval of churchmen and theologians, but did not deter other writers from joining Huxley, Leary, Alpert, and Metzner on the *yes* side of the controversy. None was more eloquent than Alan Watts, whose *Joyous Cosmology* (1962), a Zen-flavored exposition of his psychedelic experiences and their esthetic and spiritual values, immediately took its place

133

beside *The Doors of Perception* as a persuasive celebration of the chemically changed consciousness. "Despite the widespread and undiscriminating prejudice against drugs as such," he wrote, "and despite the claims of certain religious disciplines to be the sole means to genuine mystical insight, I can find no essential difference between the experiences induced, under favorable conditions, by these chemicals [LSD, mescaline, psilocybin] and the states of 'cosmic consciousness' recorded by R. M. Bucke, William James, Evelyn Underhill, Raynor Johnson, and other investigators of mysticism." In a later essay, published in 1969, he held to the same view. With reference to LSD experience that he had in 1959 under the supervision of Drs. Sterling Bunnell and Michael Agron of the Langley-Porter Clinic in San Francisco, he declared:

"In the course of two experiments I was amazed and somewhat embarrassed to find myself going through states of consciousness which corresponded precisely with every description of major mystical experiences that I had ever read. Furthermore, they exceeded both in depth and in a peculiar quality of unexpectedness the three 'natural and spontaneous' experiences of this kind which had happened to me in previous years."[29]

While writers like Watts provided this kind of personal testimony, others presented evidence gained from experimenting with psychedelics on volunteer subjects. In 1962, with the cooperation of Leary, Walter N. Pahnke, a doctoral candidate at Harvard, gave ten theological students psilocybin during a Good Friday service and obtained evidence of mystical experiences, reported by the subjects, that he regarded as statistically significant.[30] In 1964, when Sidney Cohen published his *Beyond Within*, he devoted one chapter to the question, "Model Psychosis or Instant Zen?" and concluded on the basis of his research with LSD that it could produce either a psychotic or a "visionary state"—either hell or heaven, as Huxley had indicated. Two years later R. E. L. Masters and Jean Houston reported in their *Varieties of Psychedelic Experience* that out of

134

a total of 206 psychedelic drug subjects with whom they had experimented, six had attained "the authentic and introvertive mystical state as described by Stace."[31]

If such experiments provided an abundance of ammunition for the affirmative, those on the negative side of the debate could also draw upon a growing arsenal of research and opinion published by medical authorities and social scientists. Richard Blum, consultant to the Institute for the Study of Human Problems at Stanford University, led a research team that observed and interviewed users of LSD in an effort to chart their beliefs and behavior. When he revealed his findings in *Utopiates* (1964), he presented a variety of viewpoints, including an essay by Leary, Alpert, and Metzner. But on balance the comments of the team —questioning the motives and methods of psychedelic experimenters, and speculating on the toilet training of hippie-types who shunned soap and called marijuana "pot"—weighed against the transcendental view of the psychedelics. In the end Blum remarked, "It does not appear that LSD is a short cut to personality reconstruction or to nirvana."[32]

With this Dr. Donald Louria completely agreed. Long a critic of the psychedelic enthusiasm, he summed up his indictment of it in *The Drug Scene* (1968). Medical records, he said, showed that LSD users risked such negative effects as overwhelming panic, persistent or recurrent psychosis, self-mutilation, suicide, and murder. They might, in the opinion of some researchers, incur chromosomal abnormalities. As for marijuana, a mild form of cannabis, it was less dangerous than the more potent psychedelics, yet not entirely harmless; it occasionally caused panic or psychosis. Hashish, a more powerful form of cannabis, was far more likely to produce these negative reactions. The marijuana smoker also ran the risk of becoming, not physically addicted, but psychologically dependent on the drug.

The "original notion" that LSD could induce transcendent religious experience, "has for the most part not withstood the test of time," said Louria.

It certainly is true that LSD experiences are often characterized by hallucinations and illusions which have religious overtones, but once the LSD experience is over, there is no evidence that the religous aspect of the experience has had any lasting beneficial effects on the user. By definition a transcendental experience must have profound and long-lasting influence and effect specific and positive changes in behavioral patterns. Since this has not occurred under the influence of LSD, it would seem fair to conclude that the religious aspects of the LSD trip may well be pleasurable—and to certain individuals, especially those with religious training, meaningful—but they are not, in the conventional understanding of the term, transcendental.

As a case study in the debilitating effects of drug use, Louria pointed to Haight-Ashbury. And few would deny that by 1968 the flowers had wilted: crime and disease had blighted the most famous of the Hippie centers, and many of the original dwellers were scattering to rural regions to experiment with tribal living in agrarian communes. Others were joining the international stream of Hippies migrating annually from America, England, and European countries to the Near East and India, particularly to Katmandu, whence came nightmarish stories of Hippie drug excesses and death.[33]

By this time the journalistic view of the psychedelics had taken a decidedly negative turn, and legislators had tightened the federal and state drug laws. It could not be said, at the end of the decade, that the laws were entirely wise or that the use of psychedelics, particularly marijuana, was declining. It did seem evident that many Americans regarded LSD no longer as benign but as dangerous, and that by and large they would support medical men who wanted psychedelic experimentation continued, but only by qualified, responsible researchers, under strict controls.[34]

Yet the debate over drugs and mysticism continued. In the fall of 1969 Walter Houston Clark, professor of the psychology of religion at Andover Newton Theological School, and author of the highly regarded *Psychology of Religion*, published an earnest argument for the affirmative, *Chemical Ecstasy*. Seven years previously he had requested and received LSD from Leary and had written in his report of the experiment, "I would describe the experience as a conversion experience of the most radical nature rather than a mystical experience of the classical variety as Stace has defined it. Yet, though without many of the indications of mystical experience, I know I will understand the mystics much better, having had the experience."[35] Later, in his presidential address to the Society for the Scientific Study of Religion, "The Mystical Consciousness and World Understanding," he suggested that the West could gain insight into Eastern faiths through psychedelic drugs, which "activate in many people experiences that cannot be distinguished from more regular cases of mysticism."[36] In *Chemical Ecstasy* he wrote: ". . . the drugs provide the most ready access to what William James declared was the root of religion, namely mystical experience, the most captivating and transforming experience known to man. I do not say categorically that the discovery of LSD ranks with the Copernican revolution; only that it might."

"I have tried both LSD and psilocybin several times myself," he stated. And while he conceded that psychedelics could be dangerous, he argued that the dangers had been exaggerated by those who had not investigated thoroughly and who, "above all, *have never tried the drugs themselves.* They have been content with scientific hearsay; they have refused to look through Galileo's telescope!"

Having made his own "eight-year study of the psychedelics" he was convinced that the benefits to be derived from them in religion, the rehabilitation of criminals and of alcoholics, and the treatment of mental and of terminal illness outweighed all risks and justified his plea for more flexible laws governing use of the drugs. He documented his book with scientific reports and accounts of experiments like Pahnke's Good Friday session, which he had helped to supervise, and in the end he declared, "I am not a pharmacologist but a psychologist of religion. Neither am I a mystic, but a scholar of religion and a believer in the importance of mysticism." In all it was a forceful argument by a bold thinker, yet those without Clark's firm faith in the drugs might see in it a tendency to draw sweeping conclusions from insufficient evidence. Examples of this were the metaphor of Galileo's telescope, the suggestion that the notorious Hell's Angels of Haight-Ashbury had been permanently gentled by LSD, a brief essay on the saintliness of Leary, and in similar key this passage:

"Fortunately, Socrates, Moses, Gautama, St. Francis, St. Paul and Jesus did not have a representative of the American Medical Association at their elbows when the spirit came. Perhaps the time may come when we will feel the same way about Timothy Leary."[37]

Whatever else might be said of the debate over drugs and mysticism, no one could deny that it stirred emotion.

And now, having tried to present a fair sampling of varying viewpoints in the controversy, I must state plainly what the reader must already have realized. I do not believe that chemical agents, whether those used by James and Blood, or the psychedelic drugs of the present day, can induce mystical experience as defined in the first chapter of this study. I express this view with no thought of settling the issue, but in order to explain my treatment of psychedelic experience. That is, I have devoted relatively little space to the experience and thought of Blood, Leary, and numerous other psychedelic experimenters because I do not regard it as mysticism.

I have not arrived at this position without much reflection upon Huxley's advocacy of the psychedelics, for in the course of studying his writings I have developed considerable admiration for this remarkable man. It is possible, however, that in judging these drugs he was overly influenced by his desire for deeper spiritual experience and his keen interest in new scientific discoveries. As for others in the Vedanta movement, Christopher Isherwood has not identified psychedelic experience with mystical experience, and Gerald Heard, though sympathetic toward the drugs, also stops short of doing so in his *Five Ages of Man.* [38] Prabhavananda holds that drugs cannot induce mystical experience. His statement, written for this book at my invitation, is included as Appendix A.

When certain proponents of psychedelic ecstasy, including experimental subjects who report their experiences, state that these drugs induce what they term "mystical experience," they seem to mean merely heightened sensual perception, psychological insight, or religious feeling, or a blend of the three. By my definition these are not, either singly or together, mystical experience, although it is nearly always *accompanied*, to be sure, by religious feeling. Hence I would suggest that these proponents are not speaking of mystical experience but of other forms of experience, which may, of course, be deeply moving.

Other proponents, such as Clark, identify psychedelic ecstasy with the kind of models, drawn from the writings of the world's great mystics, on which I have based my definitions of mystical experience and mysticism. I would suggest, however, that psychedelic ecstasy and mystical experience are not identical, but that they differ in significant ways.

To begin with a point noted in the first chapter, visions and voices as mystical experience are suspect. Yet personal narratives of psychedelic ecstasy—as found in the previously mentioned books of Clark, Masters and Houston, Leary, Cohen, and in *The Ecstatic Adventure* (1968), edited by Ralph Metzner—exhibit visions and voices in profusion. The subjects see myriads of visions of everything from jeweled serpents to Oriental harems to the heavenly angels and Christ. They engage in conversations and emotional debates with the figures in the visions; they enact complete dramas as they visit their childhood, their evolutionary past, Greek mythology, or the great scenes of history, especially religious history. Such happenings are presented in overwhelming detail in *Exploring Inner Space* (1961), in which "Jane Dunlap" (the pseudonym of a well-known American nutritionist) narrates her LSD experiences. She compares these to a Technicolor movie "so dramatic and emotionally packed that it claims every instant of your attention."[39]

All this leads to another distinguishing mark of the psychedelic ecstasy—its kaleidoscopic nature. The visions, voices, scenes, and moods shift constantly, and often with bewildering rapidity. Now the subject is in hell, now in heaven, now back again in hell. True, the kaleidoscope does congeal at times into experiences that the subject describes in mystical phraseology. Consider, for instance, this excerpt from the narrative of the Reverend Mary Hart, "ordained minister in a Midwest Protestant parish," whose experience under LSD is presented by both Clark and Metzner.

"Oneness. All one. In-Godness. Indescribable. Utmost. Emotionless. No self. No sensations. Self was within and without. Time gone. Space gone. Nowhere, but infinitely everywhere. No time, but eternally now. Vast oneness. In-God." And so on.

Judging by such phraseology alone, one might suppose that the Reverend Hart had mystical experience. But this is only a part of the whole. Before what seems to have been a rather extended religious and "mystical" phase, she noted, "Psychotic phase. Forms became immense machines, steel structures. . . . threatening. . . . Strong sense of insanity." Then, *after* the religious and "mystical" phase, she fell "back into the psychotic level. Far more acute than the descent into it the first time." This merged into disturbing sexual scenes, during which she expressed loathing for her guide, a veteran of psychedelic sessions who was there to help her get safely through her experience. She passed from a vision of "a brothel" into "an agony of self-loathing, shame, disgrace and guilt. I retched a dry retch. I felt slovenly and wanton. . . . My guide sensed my need. He became my priest. He forgave me and gave me absolution. I felt restored. . . . I loved him profoundly."

Then she "asked God to love him" and experienced peace and joy. She gradually emerged into reality feeling "a sense of extreme fatigue." It might also be noted that somewhere within the kaleidoscope, at an unspecified point in the sequence of phases, she found herself "in a commingling union, a conversation with William James. I loved him. I thanked him profoundly for his great book *Varieties*, which he had given me while on earth."[40]

Now, this is not an exceptional but a fairly typical narrative of psychedelic ecstasy, and I think it differs markedly, in its kaleidoscopic quality (not to mention the visions and voices), from the typical pattern of mystical experience. Compare it with the serene simplicity of Thomas Merton's descriptions of mystical experience, or with Howard Thurman's quiet meditations. Or compare the fourteenth-century Dutch mystic Jan van Ruysbroeck, who writes, "For in this unfathomable abyss of the Simplicity, all things are wrapped in fruitive bliss. . . ."[41] Simplicity —not kaleidoscopic whirl; this is one of the differences.

Alan Watts recognized this in 1958, before he became a proponent of psychedelic ecstasy. In *Nature, Man and Woman* he commented:

From personal, though limited, experimentation with a research group working with lysergic acid, I would judge that the state of consciousness induced is confused with a mystical state because of similarities of language used in describing the two. The experience is multidimensional, as if everything were inside, or implied, everything else, requiring a description which is paradoxical from the standpoint of ordinary logic. But whereas the drug gives a vision of nature which is infinitely complex, the mystical state is clarifying, and gives a vision which is as infinitely simple. The drug seems to give the intelligence a kaleidoscopic quality which "patterns" the perception of relations in accordance with its own peculiar structure.[42]

Advocates of chemical ecstasy generally agree on the need for a guide, like the man who helped Mary Hart. Otherwise the subject may have a "bad trip"—that is, experience little else besides paranoia and other wretched states. Surely this is a significant difference between psychedelic and mystical experience. The mystic does not need a companion at his elbow to keep him from lapsing into psychosis.

One reason why the psychedelic tripper needs a guide is that he is so extremely vulnerable to suggestion. The drugs seem to magnify the slightest thought, and if that happens to be religious —well and good; the drug may expand it into a magnificent vision of Christ or Buddha. But if then the memory of some unpleasant incident, or a sudden noise, or a shadow on the wall, or some other ordinarily insignificant thing should happen to trigger a negative thought, the vision may shift with quicksilver suddenness from heaven to hell, and the subject find himself struggling against psychotic fear or anger.

Quite the opposite is true of the mystical experience. It is not a state of heightened suggestibility. Instead of making the mystic vulnerable to negative thoughts, it strengthens him against them. Howard Thurman has testified eloquently to this, and, far more important, demonstrated it in his daily life. Thomas Kelly demonstrated it in the terror-laden atmosphere of Nazi Germany.

Which brings us to effects, to the test, "By their fruits ye shall know them." That mystical experience results in unselfishness, humility, moral living, loving-kindness, and constructive accomplishment has been demonstrated in the lives of men like Thurman and Kelly and Rufus Jones, not to mention the great mystics of world history. Can as much be said for psychedelic experience? Certainly not yet, it seems to me. This is not to brush aside the claims made for the therapeutic and character-building results of chemical ecstasy, but simply to say that they have not yet met the test of time. Moreover, the negative results of drug-taking as compiled by Louria and indicated by the troubles of the Hippies seem not to augur well for good fruits in the future. Neither does Leary's frenetic *High Priest*, with its opening sentence, "In the beginning was the TURN ON," its aura of alcohol, sex, and unrestrained drug usage, and its final episode, in which Leary, driving a car after a psychedelic drug session, has to resist the impulse to swerve, with his two passengers, over a cliff.

It is almost as though Leary is saying, despite himself, that the fruits of psychedelic experience can be bitter indeed.

CHAPTER 8

The Mystical Strand

"There is a widespread idea current in the world that 'America' is a word synonymous with 'practicality,'" Rufus Jones remarked in 1930. "It is assumed that we are dollar-chasers pure and simple, and are interested only in what we can get our hands on, to have and to hold. There are such Americans no doubt, and there are persons with like propensities in other countries and on other continents." But nobody knew the United States who viewed it simply as a land of greedy materialism: in the "composite blood" of its people were also idealism and spirituality. Indeed, Jones went on to argue, "there has always been an important mystical strand in the life and thought of America."[1]

The importance of this strand in the twentieth century is shown, I think, by the writings of all the mystics, from Charles A. Bennett to Philip Kapleau, that we have studied in the preceding chapters. In these final pages I shall try to sum up our findings and to suggest in some measure the influence of mystical seeking upon life in modern America.

It seems to me that quantitatively these writings form a more considerable body of literature than has been generally realized, even though I have tried to select only the more important writers, and only those who appear to be within the mainstream of mysticism. If we were to pursue this subject into realms where mysticism blurs into New Thought or poetry into verse, where

143

books become booklets or pamphlets, or take the form of little-known reminiscences or forgotten studies, we should find many another mystical gleam. This transcendent brightness, so to speak, flashes out from the pages of Margaret Prescott Montague's brief essay on her mystical experience, *Twenty Minutes of Reality* (1917), and touches occasional passages in Irene Hunter's anthology, *American Mystical Verse* (1925). It gleams also in William Atzbaugh's *Seek Ye the Christ* (1949), in Frank C. Laubach's *Letters by a Modern Mystic* (1937), and in Charles Morris Addison's engaging though now seldom-read study, *The Theory and Practice of Mysticism* (1918).

Quantity alone would be relatively unimportant were it not for the quality, the high intellectual level, that on the whole distinguishes the main body of mystical literature that we have examined. True, its producers cannot be called thinkers or mystics of the first rank. Among them we find no Shankara, no Eckhart. But we do find exceptionally gifted intellectuals, cogent philosophers, sensitive artists in language. When men of this caliber write mystical thought, it is well worth reading and pondering.

The rationalist, of course, will never approve of the fact that these unorthodox thinkers advocate mystical insight as the way to ultimate truth. But we have noted repeatedly that in doing so they do not scorn reason. On the contrary they test and interpret mystical insight in the light of reason, and they argue their theology and their social criticism with forceful logic. They give final allegiance not to the irrational but to what Rudolf Otto, in his *Idea of the Holy*, calls "the non-rational or supra-rational elements in religion."[2] This is well worth remembering when voices of unreason rise around us, and words like "mystic" or "mystical" are misused to explain or justify irrational acts of violence. Such acts are foreign to the nature of the mystic. As we have seen, he is both religious—Rufus Jones knew what he was about when he identified mysticism with religion—and ethical. The mystic characteristically engages in moral preparation for his transcendent experience and follows it with efforts to attain ever higher moral standards. His experience of the divine seems to flower within this moral context and to vanish outside it. To be sure, the experience is no guarantee that he will never fall into violence or other forms of evil toward others, but it does seem to strengthen his desire not to do so.

No doubt the reader has noticed that the great majority of the mystics we have studied were born outside the United States: immigration has enriched mysticism in America just as, continuously, through the centuries, it has enhanced other aspects of American culture. Yet the lives and the thought of Rufus Jones and Thomas Kelly, of Howard Thurman, Ruth Sasaki, and Philip Kapleau, remind us that the mystic is also indigenous to twentieth-century America. Considering that outstanding mystics have immigrated to this country, or sojourned here at length as in the case of Suzuki, considering that other mystics have sprung from the native soil, and that native, immigrant, and sojourner alike have flourished here, one might well reach the conclusion that America since 1900 has been rather hospitable toward mysticism. My own view, paralleling that of Rufus Jones, is that the complex civilization of the United States cannot be summed up in a word like "materialistic"—nor in many words. Here, as in other lands, materialist and mystic and adherents of numerous other creeds live side by side. The mystical strand is certainly not dominant, but it is very much in evidence. It forms, I think, a dimension of American intellectual and religious life that is well worth further study by historians.

Some day we may hope to have much fuller historical knowledge than is now available on the organizations that have advanced Oriental mysticism in the United States. Since this study deals essentially with mystical ideas rather than mystical movements, I have no more than suggested the organizational dimensions of Vedanta and Zen. Vedanta, especially, has had a more complex history in the United States than I have indicated; for while there has been, strictly speaking, only one Vedanta movement, initiated by Vivekananda and carried on today by Vedanta centers like the one in Hollywood, there have been other organizations teaching basically Vedantic religious philosophy.[3] The most important of these is the Self-Realization Fellowship.

Established in Los Angeles in 1925 by Swami, later Parama-hansa, Yogananda, author of the extraordinary *Autobiography of a Yogi* (1946), the Fellowship teaches Vedanta with an admixture of Christianity. Its Mount Washington Center in Los Angeles is today the international headquarters of a far-flung organization; it has an Indian branch, the Yogoda Satsanga Society, founded in India by Yogananda in 1917, and its centers and meditation groups can be found in major cities around the world. In Southern California, the Fellowship also maintains four churches, two in Los Angeles, one in Fullerton, and another in San Diego. The religious services emphasize the importance of yogic meditation.[4]

In this context of the institutional basis of mysticism we might also note a development in American Catholicism that occurred at the end of the second world war when, in the words of John Tracy Ellis, "hundreds of young Americans began pouring into contemplative monasteries, many of the newcomers fresh from their service with the armed forces." Thomas Merton in his *Waters of Siloe* called attention to this movement, and Ellis suggested that it might have gained some impetus from Merton's *Seven Storey Mountain.* "What is perhaps more remarkable," he commented in 1956, "is the fact that after a decade the trend shows no signs of abating, and today the eleven Trappist monasteries in the United States are crowded with a membership of over 1,000 monks. Moreover, five years ago the first house of American Carthusians, the strictest of all the Church's religious orders, was opened near Whitingham, Vermont." After a second decade and more had passed, *Time* magazine reported, in February 1968, that the upward trend had changed into decline. As reasons for this it pointed to newcomers' impatience with the strict rules of the orders, and the development of what superiors of the contemplative societies called "today's 'Peace Corps mentality'—the desire of many young Catholics to serve God by good deeds in the world rather than through a life of prayer." The decline was also evident in France. It may have been related, in some degree, to the more general crisis that beset the Church in the sixties.[5]

Doubtless the most unlikely institution to harbor mysticism in this decade was the American college. Long had it been a citadel of secularization. Then, rather suddenly it seemed, college and university students interested in Zen and Vedanta and the novels of Hermann Hesse began taking informal, student-taught courses in mystical meditation and forming groups to practice what they learned. College teachers responded with courses in mysticism, and even meditation entered the curriculum. Those involved in all this were still, of course, a minority; yet it seemed that never before had the mystical strand been so discernible in American college and university life.

Collegiate interest in the mystical way began to take on aspects of a new fad in the late sixties, when Maharishi Mahesh Yogi of India drew an outburst of publicity as the "guru" of famous figures in the popular entertainment world, including the American motion-picture actress Mia Farrow and the British singing group, the Beatles. The Maharishi taught a simple technique of inner seeking that he called "Transcendental Meditation," and offered the American collegian the opportunity to learn it by paying a "donation" of $35 and joining his Students' International Meditation Society, which had national headquarters in Los Angeles. By February 1968, *Look* magazine said, "over 5,000 students" in the United States had "turned into transcendental meditators." By August, a nationally syndicated news service put the number at 12,000. Though the Maharishi required remarkably little self-discipline, proclaiming rather a hedonistic philosophy, "Enjoy what you are," he did state that abstention from drug-taking was essential to his method. Perhaps not surprisingly, a number of students who replaced LSD or marijuana with silent, relaxed introspection reported that they were feeling better and functioning more efficiently.[6]

Collegians were not the only element in what one newswriter called "the meditation explosion." The nation's affluent adolescents, constantly pressured by astute advertisers and publicity agents toward conformist behavior, had previously been led toward psychedelic drugs by the Beatles and other rock music artists, and now many young teen-agers followed their leaders into the lotus posture. Nor were their elders immune to the new excitement. The glare of publicity suddenly revealed any number of lesser Maharishis in places like New York City, many of them attracting disciples from a variety of age groups. *Life* magazine, after surveying the international scene from India to London, to Boston, New York and Los Angeles, was moved in February 1968 to proclaim the "Year of the Guru."[7]

It was difficult to determine—as it has always been difficult to determine such matters, whether in America or India—which of these self-proclaimed gurus were honest teachers of Hindu wisdom and which were charlatans. Time might winnow them to some extent. Meanwhile it was easy to laugh at all of them, as the press tended to do, and to dismiss the total mass of their followers as faddists. Yet surely, among the followers at least, there were sincere religious seekers. And while in one sense their enthusiasm demonstrated the power of publicity, in another it might be considered further evidence of the persistent American quest for the mystical. Though what was found might not be truly mystical, authentic mystical experience was what many sought. Clearly, too, they sought it within Oriental mystical traditions (which may have seemed exotically new) rather than within those of the West. It might well be a significant coincidence that on the very same day, February 9, 1968, that *Life* proclaimed the "Year of the Guru," *Time* reported the decline of numbers in the Catholic contemplative orders.

The Protestant faiths, to be sure, had their own issues in the sixties. One group of American theologians announced that God was dead, but the resultant controversy did not seem to affect interest in mysticism. Neither did the arguments of theologians who held that long-continuing trends such as urbanization had thoroughly secularized America.[8] Granted that proponents of this view advanced it with perceptive sociological analysis, it might still be suggested that they paid insufficient attention to the mystical strand in American life and thought.

In this chapter I have given the term "mystical strand" a broader meaning, perhaps, than Rufus Jones intended, and have applied it to diverse elements. Within it, so to speak, we find in twentieth-century America the near-mystical and the pseudo-mystical, the initiators and followers of the fads and the popular enthusiasms. We also find philosophers and theologians who comment upon mysticism, and literary artists who employ mystical ideas for esthetic purposes—poets like Allen Ginsberg and Gary Snyder, writers of fiction like J. D. Salinger. All these, in their various ways, help to disseminate mystical ideas, thus broadening the cultural impact of mysticism.

At the very center of the strand the true mystic lives and moves and has his being. If he is a gifted thinker and writer he may produce books like those that form the main body of literature that we have explored. If he is not, he may remain silent. Rufus Jones declared: "There are hundreds of mute and unnamed mystics for every one who writes a book. In fact, the most important interpreters of mysticism in all periods are those persons who quietly practice the presence of God in their daily lives without even being conscious that they are rare and unusual persons and often without knowing the meaning of the word 'mystic.' "[9] Jones delighted in meeting such persons, and, as we have seen, so also did Thomas Kelly.

But of course it is the articulate mystic, the writer like Jones himself, who has done most to make America aware of mysticism. And undeniably this kind of mystical intellectual is an extraordinary being, not only a speaker of paradox but an embodiment of paradox. In one respect, his lack of provincialism—his sensitivity to international currents of thought, his vision of the worldwide brotherhood of man—he is quite up-to-date; but in other ways, from the viewpoint of the sophisticated skeptic, he is an anachronism. While the tides of secularization rise all around him, he sits quietly seeking spiritual awakening. While louder voices than his preach self-indulgence, he continues to advocate self-naughting, self-discipline, even a certain degree of asceticism. Surely he must be doomed to extinction! Surely the center of the mystical strand will fall apart, and the secular city of the future will see no more Kellys or Mertons, no more Heschels or Thurmans or Prabhavanandas.

So the skeptic might think. But he might be wrong. History suggests that the mystic is as old as man, and that as he has endured in the past so will he continue to endure, in America as elsewhere. And because times of war and social turmoil like the present reveal with shocking clarity the transience of material things and turn men to inner seeking, we may see more, not less, mysticism. In any event, I hazard the guess that as long as there is a corner in which to meditate the mystic will be there. Silently he will go within, and joyfully he will emerge with his perennial message: all is Love; all is well.

God and Drugs

By Swami Prabhavananda

Psychedelic drugs have been known to the people of India for centuries. Although the use of such drugs is generally tolerated there, those who take them are looked down upon by the public and universally shunned by holy men and women. Of course, it is no secret that these drugs do produce psychic visions and experiences—even certain powers. In fact, Patanjali, the father of Indian Yoga, has explicitly stated that "psychic powers may be obtained by means of drugs." But he also strongly warned that the use of such means can obstruct spiritual progress and block genuine spiritual experiences. However, it is easy to be fooled into thinking that hallucinogenic drugs can produce a true experience of God. The user of LSD may actually see a light enveloping the universe or sense the presence of God or a divine being. But as soon as the effects of the drug wear off, he finds himself spiritually dry and empty. His experience is of no more consequence than a dream. God is as distant as ever. The simple but powerful language of the Bible expresses it succinctly: "By their fruits ye shall know them." This is the basis for the evaluation of a spiritual experience.

Samadhi or transcendental consciousness totally transforms a

151

man. In that ecstatic moment, experienced by one whose heart is purified, man's very Self is revealed. He at last realizes that highest wisdom known to the world's saints and sages. Are we then so naïve and foolish as to believe that such a profound experience as this can be produced by swallowing a drug? May God be bought so cheaply? In this same sense, Swami Vivekananda once compared deep (dreamless) sleep and samadhi: "If a fool goes into deep sleep, he comes out a fool; but if a fool goes into samadhi, he comes out a wise man." And in describing his own experience of samadhi, the ancient seer-philosopher Shankara wrote: "The ocean of Brahman is full of nectar—the joy of the Atman. The treasure I have found there cannot be described in words. The mind cannot conceive of it. My mind fell like a hailstone into that vast expanse of Brahman's ocean. Touching one drop of it, I melted away and became one with Brahman. And now, *though I return to human consciousness, I abide in the joy of the Atman* [italics mine]."

Even a sincere aspirant may be deceived into thinking he has experienced God. Once a friend of mine renounced the world and went to a place of retreat in the Himalayas. After being there for a few months, he wrote me a letter in which he said he had experienced samadhi. I happened to be with my Master at the time, who knew this man. I told him about the letter. "Why, I saw him only ten days ago," my Master said. "I remember looking at his eyes; there was no evidence of any samadhi. He must have seen some light and thought that vision to be samadhi." He looked at me and added, "Is it so easy to attain samadhi?" Then he quoted a verse from the Upanishads: "The knot of the heart, which is ignorance, is loosed, all doubts are dissolved, all effects of deeds destroyed, when he who is both far and near is realized."

To my mind, that statement best expresses the distinction between truth and error, between knowledge of God and the experience of psychic phenomena.

In conclusion , let me quote from the Katha Upanishad: "The mortal in whose heart desire is dead becomes immortal. The mortal in whose heart the knots of ignorance are untied becomes immortal. These are the highest truths taught in the Scriptures." Now I ask, can anyone who gains any experience through the use of drugs, claim such a transformation? Many cases are known in which a man, as he continues to use drugs, deteriorates physically and mentally. This certainly is not characteristic of a genuine spiritual experience.

Vedanta and the Problem of Evil

By Swami Prabhavananda

According to Advaita Vedanta, the universe of appearance has only an empirical reality. Our experience of this universe with all its joys and sorrows, with all its so-called good and evil is a misreading of the Reality which is Brahman. Brahman appearing through time, space, and relativity (maya) appears as this universe. To quote Shankara: "Brahman is the ground and the reality. This appearance of a universe is only seen through our deluded eyes. When true knowledge arises, Brahman, which is one with Atman, is revealed as existence itself, and the apparent universe cannot be seen apart from it. You may mistake a rope for a snake, if you are deluded. But, when the delusion passes, you realize that the imagined snake was none other than the rope. So also this universe is none other than Brahman."

As one enters into samadhi the universe of appearance vanishes. The seer then declares in the words of Shankara: "Where is this universe? Who took it away? Has it merged into something else? A while ago, I beheld it—now it exists no longer. Here is the Ocean of Brahman, full of endless joy. How can I accept or reject anything? Is there anything apart from Brahman?"

Once in course of a discussion with a brother disciple of mine, I remarked that Brahman is only experienced in samadhi, and not when one comes back to the normal plane. My master overheard our discussion and he came out of his room and said to me, "Ah! You have become omniscient!" I enquired, "But is it possible to see God while in the normal state also?" To that he replied out of the fullness of his own experience, "Show me the line of demarcation where matter ends and Spirit begins."

In this connection, let me again quote Shankara: "Our perception of the universe is a continuous perception of Brahman, though the ignorant man is not aware of this. Indeed, this universe is nothing but Brahman. See Brahman everywhere, under all circumstances, with the eye of the spirit and a tranquil heart. How can the physical eyes see anything but physical objects? How can the mind of the enlightened man think of anything other than the Reality?"

Swami Vivekananda once remarked to a disciple: The first experience in samadhi is "the world is not, God is." Then comes the experience, "God is all." In the words of Shankara, "with the eye of the spirit, he sees all as Brahman."

Notes

CHAPTER 1. GROUND FOR EXPLORATION

1. Of course, American scholars have not completely ignored the subject of mysticism in America. Examples of general
and specialized works that take cognizance of it are Merle Curti,
The Growth of American Thought (3d ed.; New York: Harper &
Row, 1964); Robert E. Spiller and others, eds., *Literary History
of the United States*, 2 vols. (3d ed. rev.; New York: The Macmil-
lan Co., 1963); James Ward Smith and A. Leland Jamison, eds.,
Religion in American Life, 3 vols. (Princeton, N.J.: Princeton
University Press, 1961); Arthur Christy, *The Orient in American
Transcendentalism* (New York: Columbia University Press,
1932); Van Meter Ames, *Zen and American Thought* (Honolulu:
University of Hawaii Press, 1962); Herbert Wallace Schneider,
Religion in 20th Century America (rev. ed.; New York:
Atheneum, 1964, paperback); Henry F. May, *The End of Ameri-
can Innocence: A Study of the First Years of Our Own Time
1912–1917* (New York: Alfred A. Knopf, 1959).

2. See Rufus M. Jones, *Studies in Mystical Religion* (London: Macmillan & Co., 1909) and *New Studies in Mystical Religion* (New York: The Macmillan Co., 1927); Evelyn Underhill,

Mysticism: A Study in the Nature and Development of Man's Spiritual Consciousness (12th ed.; New York: Meridian Books, 1955, paperback); W. T. Stace, *Mysticism and Philosophy* (Philadelphia: J. B. Lippincott Co., 1960) and *The Teachings of the Mystics* (New York: Mentor Books, 1960, paperback).

3. For quoted passages see Margaret Smith, trans. and ed., *Readings from the Mystics of Islam* (London: Luzac & Co., 1950), pp. 65, 70–71.

4. Plotinus, *The Enneads*, Stephen MacKenna, trans., and B. S. Page, rev. (3d ed.; London: Faber & Faber, 1962), p. 624.

5. *Meister Eckhart*, Raymond Bernard Blakney, trans. (New York: Harper Torchbooks, 1957, paperback), p. 131.

6. Eckhart is quoted in Rudolph Otto, *Mysticism East and West*, Bertha L. Bracey and Richenda C. Payne, trans. (New York: Collier Books, 1962, paperback), p. 80. On Blake see *The Complete Writings*, Geoffrey Keynes, ed. (London: Nonesuch Press, 1957), p. 431.

7. Stace, *Mysticism and Philosophy*, p. 67.

8. New York: The Macmillan Co., 1920, p. 339.

9. *The Confessions*, E. B. Pusey, trans. (New York: E. P. Dutton & Co., 1951), pp. 145–46.

10. Swami Prabhavananda, *The Spiritual Heritage of India* (New York: Doubleday–Anchor Books, 1964, paperback), p. 346.

11. *Complete Works*, E. Allison Peers, trans. and ed. (Westminster, Md.: Newman Bookshop, 1946), II, 87.

12. Underhill, p. 201.

13. For the naturalistic interpretation, see Alfred P. Stiernotte, ed., *Mysticism and the Modern Mind* (New York: Liberal Arts Press, 1959), especially pp. 5–6, 38, 147–48.

14. For the best discussion of this, see Stace, *Mysticism and Philosophy*, pp. 47–51.

15. Sigmund Freud, *Complete Psychological Works* (stand. ed.; London: Hogarth Press and the Institute of Psycho-analysis, 1961), XXI, 72–73.

16. George Santayana, *The Life of Reason*, III: *Reason in Religion* (New York: Charles Scribner's Sons, 1905), p. 277;

Bertrand Russell, *Mysticism and Logic and Other Essays* (London: George Allen & Unwin, 1917), pp. 1–32.

17. Richard Maurice Bucke, *Cosmic Consciousness: A Study in the Evolution of the Human Mind* (New York: E. P. Dutton & Co., 1923), pp. 1–3, 7, 10, 67.

CHAPTER 2. EXPERIMENTS IN PHILOSOPHY

1. Gay Wilson Allen, *William James: A Biography* (New York: Viking Press, 1967), pp. 408–415, 423.

2. *The Varieties of Religious Experience* (New York: Modern Library, 1929), p. 370; William James, *Letters*, Henry James, ed. (Boston: Atlantic Monthly Press, 1920), II, 210, 211; Ralph Barton Perry, *The Thought and Character of William James* (Boston: Little, Brown & Co., 1935), II, 677.

3. *Letters*, II, 76–77.

4. Allen, p. 391.

5. *Varieties*, pp. 371–73, 377–78, 417.

6. "A Suggestion about Mysticism," *Journal of Philosophy*, VII (February 17, 1910), 85.

7. *Varieties*, pp. 370, 415, 417, 505–509.

8. Unsigned review article, *Atlantic Monthly*, XXXIV (November, 1874), 628; see also Perry, I, 727, *n.* 20. Blood's pamphlet was issued in Amsterdam, N.Y. in 1874; the quoted passage is on pp. 33–34.

9. William James, "On Some Hegelisms," *Mind*, VII (April, 1882), 206–208; *Letters*, II, 37.

10. *Varieties*, pp. 377–82, 561.

11. Perry, II, 225, 228, 554, *n.* 2; see also H. M. Kallen's Introduction to Blood's *Pluriverse: An Essay in the Philosophy of Pluralism* (London: Kegan Paul, Trench, Trubner & Co., 1920), p. xxii.

12. William James, "A Pluralistic Mystic," *Hibbert Journal*, VIII, (July, 1910), 740.

13. Blood, *Anaesthetic Revelation*, pp. 13, 31, 33–36.

14. *Pluriverse*, pp. viii-ix, 69, 239, 244.

15. William Ernest Hocking in his Preface to Bennett's *Dilemma of Religious Knowledge* (New Haven: Yale University Press, 1931).

16. Rufus M. Jones in his Preface to Bennett's *A Philosophical Study of Mysticism* (New Haven: Yale University Press, 1931), p. ix.

17. *Dilemma,* pp. 10, 119.

18. *Philosophical Study,* pp. 7, 9, 10–11, 20, 26, 28.

19. *Ibid.,* pp. 115–38.

20. *Ibid.,* pp. 27, 74, 75.

21. *Ibid.,* pp. 19, 162.

22. *Ibid.,* pp. 108–110.

23. *Ibid.,* p. 6.

24. *Varieties,* p. 446.

CHAPTER 3. QUAKER LIGHTS

1. See Howard Haines Brinton, *Friends for 300 Years: The History and Beliefs of the Society of Friends since George Fox Started the Quaker Movement* (New York: Harper & Brothers, 1952).

2. Chicago: Willett, Clark & Co., 1936, pp. 120–21.

3. Rufus M. Jones, "Why I Enroll with the Mystics," *Contemporary American Theology: Theological Autobiographies,* Vergilius Ferm, ed., I (New York: Round Table Press, 1932), 196–97; Elizabeth Gray Vining, *Rufus Jones: Friend of Life* (Philadelphia: J. B. Lippincott Co., 1958), pp. 85–86.

4. "Why I Enroll," p. 207.

5. Rufus M. Jones, *The Trail of Life in College* (New York: The Macmillan Co., 1929), p. 160.

6. "Why I Enroll," pp. 206–209; Vining, pp. 99, 200–201.

7. Vining, pp. 108, 142, 331–33.

8. Rufus M. Jones, *Studies in Mystical Religion* (London: Macmillan & Co., 1909), p. xv; *The Luminous Trail* (New York: The Macmillan Co., 1947), pp. 25–26; Vining, p. 251.

9. Rufus M. Jones, *Social Law in the Spiritual World* (New

York: George H. Doran Co., 1923), pp. 97 ff., quotation p. 99 *n.;* "Why I Enroll," p. 196; *The Testimony of the Soul* (New York: The Macmillan Co., 1936), pp. 59–61, 71, 86–87.

10. Rufus M. Jones, *New Studies in Mystical Religion* (New York: The Macmillan Co., 1927), p. 177; *Pathways to the Reality of God* (New York: The Macmillan Co., 1931), p. 61; "Why I Enroll," p. 213.

11. *Pathways*, pp. 48–49; *Luminous Trail*, pp. 19–20.

12. *Pathways*, p. 141; Vining, p. 258; Jones, "Why I Enroll," pp. 213–14.

13. "Why I Enroll," pp. 212–13; James H. Leuba, *The Psychology of Religious Mysticism* (New York: Harcourt, Brace & Co., 1926), p. 46; Jones, *New Studies*, pp. 9–14.

14. Leuba, chaps. VIII and IX, quotation p. 191; Jones, *Studies*, pp. xvii–xviii; *New Studies*, pp. 9, 29–31.

15. Rufus M. Jones, *The Flowering of Mysticism* (New York: The Macmillan Co., 1939), pp. 5–6.

16. Jones, *New Studies*, pp. 19–20, 150; *Some Exponents of Mystical Religion* (New York: Abingdon Press, 1930), p. 42; *Testimony*, pp. 160–61.

17. Rufus M. Jones, *A Call to What Is Vital* (New York: The Macmillan Co., 1948), pp. 64–65; Vining, pp. 258–60.

18. See James, *Varieties*, p. 407; Jones, "Why I Enroll," pp. 199–203, and *Spiritual Reformers in the Sixteenth and Seventeenth Centuries* (London: Macmillan & Co., 1914), pp. xxv–xxviii.

19. "Why I Enroll," pp. 203–206; *Social Law*, pp. 135, 137, 138.

20. *Luminous Trail*, pp. 11–13, 15–25; *Social Law*, p. 138.

21. "Why I Enroll," p. 211.

22. Rufus M. Jones, *Fundamental Ends of Life* (New York: The Macmillan Co., 1924), pp. 102, 103; *New Studies*, p. 90.

23. For biographical facts on Kelly see the Biographical Memoir by Douglas V. Steere in Thomas Raymond Kelly, *A Testament of Devotion* (New York: Harper & Brothers, 1941)—hereafter cited as *Testament*—pp. 1–18, and Richard M. Kelly,

Thomas Kelly: A Biography (New York: Harper & Row, 1966)
—hereafter cited as RMK, *Kelly*—pp. 21–91, quotation p. 91.

24. RMK, *Kelly*, p. 102; *Testament*, pp. 18–19.

25. RMK, *Kelly*, pp. 94–109, quotation p. 106.

26. *Testament*, p. 21.

27. RMK, *Kelly*, pp. 92–93, 122.

28. Thomas Raymond Kelly, *Reality of the Spiritual World* (Wallingford, Pa.: Pendle Hill, 1944), p. 53.

29. See RMK, *Kelly*, pp. 24, 45, 70, 73, 116, and *Testament*, pp. 8, 18–19.

30. *Testament*, pp. 56, 92, 93–95; *Reality*, pp. 31–32.

31. Thomas Raymond Kelly, *The Eternal Promise*, Richard M. Kelly, ed. (New York: Harper & Row, 1966), pp. 72–80.

32. *Reality*, pp. 19–22.

33. *Eternal Promise*, pp. 87–88; *Testament*, p. 61.

34. *Eternal Promise*, p. 25; RMK, *Kelly*, p. 102; *Testament*, pp. 56, 61–62.

35. *Testament*, p. 21; see also RMK, *Kelly*, pp. 97, 99, 109.

36. *Eternal Promise*, pp. 30–31, 41–43; *Testament*, p. 68.

37. *Testament*, pp. 89, 91, 102, 108–109.

38. *Testament*, pp. 38–45, 120–21; *Reality*, pp. 41–52.

39. *Reality*, pp. 54, 55–56, 59, 60; *Testament*, pp. 77, 81, 82, 88.

CHAPTER 4. THREE VARIETIES OF MYSTICISM

1. Howard Thurman, *Mysticism and the Experience of Love*, Pendle Hill Pamphlet No. 115 (Wallingford, Pa.: Pendle Hill, 1961), pp. 4–5.

2. Elizabeth Yates, *Howard Thurman: Portrait of a Practical Dreamer* (New York: John Day Co., 1964), pp. 38–39.

3. *Ibid.*, pp. 80–84.

4. Howard Thurman, *Disciplines of the Spirit* (New York: Harper & Row, 1963), p. 96.

5. Yates, p. 84.

6. Howard Thurman, *Deep Is the Hunger: Meditations for Apostles of Sensitiveness* (New York: Harper & Brothers, 1951), pp. 169–70.

7. Howard Thurman, *The Inward Journey* (New York: Harper & Brothers, 1961), pp. 135–36.

8. *Mysticism*, pp. 3, 6.

9. Howard Thurman, *Meditations of the Heart* (New York: Harper & Brothers, 1953), p. 174, and *The Creative Encounter: An Interpretation of Religion and the Social Witness* (New York: Harper & Brothers, 1954), p. 75.

10. *Meditations of the Heart*, pp. 104, 110–11.

11. Howard Thurman, *Jesus and the Disinherited* (New York: Abingdon-Cokesbury Press, 1949), pp. 13–14.

12. *Ibid.*, p. 98.

13. Lerone Bennett, Jr., *What Manner of Man: A Biography of Martin Luther King, Jr.* (Chicago: Johnson Publishing Co., 1964), pp. 74–75.

14. *Jesus and the Disinherited*, p. 98.

15. See Howard Thurman, *Footprints of a Dream: The Story of the Church for the Fellowship of All Peoples* (New York: Harper & Brothers, 1959).

16. Yates, pp. 127, 128.

17. *Ibid.*, pp. 98, 100, 104–109, 129, 179.

18. Howard Thurman, *The Luminous Darkness: A Personal Interpretation of the Anatomy of Segregation and the Ground of Hope* (New York: Harper & Row, 1965), p. 30.

19. *Ibid.*, p. 5.

20. *Ibid.*, pp. 104, 106–107.

21. *Ibid.*, p. x.

22. Jacob J. Petuchowski, "Faith as the Leap of Action: The Theology of Abraham Joshua Heschel," *Commentary*, XXV (May, 1958), 390.

23. Chap. 19 of *The Jews*, Louis Finkelstein, ed. (3d ed.; New York: Harper & Brothers, 1960), II.

24. See E. LaB. Cherbonnier, "A. J. Heschel and the Philoso-

phy of the Bible: Mystic or Rationalist?" *Commentary*, XXVII (January, 1959), 23–29.

25. Gershom G. Scholem, *Major Trends in Jewish Mysticism* (3d rev. ed.; New York: Shocken Books, 1954), pp. 15–16.

26. Abraham Joshua Heschel, *Man Is Not Alone* (New York: Farrar, Straus & Young, 1951), p. 169.

27. Abraham Joshua Heschel, *God in Search of Man* (New York: Farrar, Straus & Cudahy, 1955), p. 138.

28. *Man Is Not Alone*, pp. 77–78.

29. *Ibid.*, pp. 59, 64, 67.

30. Abraham Joshua Heschel, *The Insecurity of Freedom: Essays on Human Existence* (New York: Farrar, Straus & Giroux, 1966), pp. 117–19; see also *God in Search of Man*, pp. 7–8.

31. Bertrand Russell, *Mysticism and Logic and Other Essays* (London: George Allen & Unwin, 1917), p. 8.

32. P. 67.

33. P. 131.

34. *Man Is Not Alone,*. pp. 171–73.

35. *Ibid.*, pp. 244–45; Abraham Joshua Heschel, *The Prophets* (New York: Harper & Row, 1962), chap. 12.

36. *Man Is Not Alone*, pp. 245, 269; Martin Buber, *Hasidism and Modern Man*, Maurice Friedman, ed. and trans. (New York: Horizon Press, 1958), p. 49.

37. *God In Search of Man*, p. 200 (the quotation of Eckhart is on pp. 205–206); see also Abraham Joshua Heschel, *The Sabbath: Its Meaning for Modern Man* (New York: Farrar, Straus & Young, 1951), pp. 7 ff.

38. Thomas Merton, *The Seven Storey Mountain* (New York: Signet Books, 1952, paperback), pp. 278–79.

39. Thomas Merton, *New Seeds of Contemplation* (Norfolk, Conn.: New Directions, 1961), pp. 147–48.

40. Thomas Merton, *The Living Bread* (New York: Farrar, Straus & Cudahy, 1956), p. 50; *The Sign of Jonas* (New York: Harcourt, Brace & Co., 1953), p. 198; *Selected Poems* (enlarged ed.; New York: New Directions, 1967, paperback), p. 68.

41. *New Seeds of Contemplation*, pp. 182, 226–28.

CHAPTER 5. VEDANTA

1. Christopher Isherwood, *Ramakrishna and His Disciples* (New York: Simon & Schuster, 1965), pp. 318–25; Wendell Thomas, *Hinduism Invades America* (New York: Beacon Press, 1930), chap. 4; Swami Nikhilananda, *Vivekananda: A Biography* (New York: Ramakrishna–Vivekananda Center, 1953), pp. 56–98, 150–59.

2. Christopher Isherwood, "Introduction," and Swami Prabhavananda, "The Yoga of Meditation," in *Vedanta for the Western World*, Christopher Isherwood, ed. (New York: Compass Books, 1960, paperback), pp. 1, 80–88; T. M. P. Mahadevan, "Western Vedanta," in *Vedanta for Modern Man*, Christopher Isherwood, ed. (New York: Harper & Brothers, 1951), pp. 15–19. On the relationship of the Vedanta and the Yoga to the Six Systems of Hindu thought see Sarvepalli Radhakrishnan, *Indian Philosophy* (2d ed. rev.; New York: The Macmillan Co., 1931), II, 17–28.

3. Swami Prabhavananda, *The Spiritual Heritage of India* (New York: Doubleday–Anchor Books, 1964, paperback), p. 329; Swami Nikhilananda, *Hinduism: Its Meaning for the Liberation of the Spirit* (New York: Harper & Brothers, 1958), pp. 14–17.

4. Prabhavananda, *Spiritual Heritage*, p. 60.

5. Nikhilananda, *Hinduism*, pp. 125–26.

6. Sir Charles Eliot, *Hinduism and Buddhism* (London: Routledge & Kegan Paul, 1921), II, 307.

7. *Spiritual Heritage*, p. v.

8. Swami Prabhavananda, *The Sermon on the Mount According to Vedanta* (Hollywood: Vedanta Press, 1964), p. 64, as revised by Prabhavananda in statement to me, December 1967.

9. *Ibid.*, p. 14.

10. Isherwood, *Ramakrishna*, p. 2; also *An Approach to Vedanta* (Hollywood: Vedanta Press, 1963), p. 46.

11. Christopher Isherwood, *The World in the Evening* (New York: Random House, 1954), pp. 94–95, 234–36, 285–86, 292–93.

12. Christopher Isherwood, *A Meeting by the River* (New York: Simon & Schuster, 1967), p. 173.

13. Gerald Heard, "Vedanta and Western History," in Isherwood, ed., *Vedanta for Modern Man*, p. 11. See also Isherwood, *Approach to Vedanta*, p. 15.

14. Gerald Heard, *A Preface to Prayer* (New York: Harper & Brothers, 1944), p. 97.

15. Gerald Heard, *Pain, Sex and Time* (New York: Harper & Brothers, 1939), p. 173 *et passim*.

16. Gerald Heard, *The Code of Christ* (New York: Harper & Brothers, 1941), p. 32; *The Creed of Christ* (New York: Harper & Brothers, 1940), pp. 11–15.

17. Gerald Heard, *The Eternal Gospel* (New York: Harper & Brothers, 1946), pp. 227–28.

18. See Heard, *Creed*, pp. 145, 148–54, 160–61; *Pain, Sex and Time*, pp. 174, 198; *Preface to Prayer*, chap. 7; *Is God in History?* (New York: Harper & Brothers, 1950), p. 175.

19. Heard, *Pain, Sex and Time*, p. 203; *The Source of Civilization* (New York: Harper & Brothers, 1937), p. 229; *Preface to Prayer*, pp. 51, 151, 162–64.

20. Isherwood in *Aldous Huxley 1894–1963: A Memorial Volume*, Julian Huxley, ed. (London: Chatto & Windus, 1965), p. 158; Heard, *ibid.*, p. 104.

21. Aldous Huxley, *The Doors of Perception* and *Heaven and Hell* (New York: Harper Colophon Books, 1963, paperback), p. 41.

22. Founded in 1938, the magazine during its first three years was entitled *The Voice of India*. Selections of essays by Huxley, Heard, and others have been published in the two previously cited volumes edited by Christopher Isherwood, *Vedanta for Modern Man* (New York: Harper & Brothers, 1951) and *Vedanta for the Western World* (New York: Compass Books, 1960, paperback), hereafter cited as *VWW*.

23. Aldous Huxley, *Time Must Have a Stop* (New York: Harper & Brothers, 1944), pp. 293–95; see also *VWW*, pp. 33–34.

24. Aldous Huxley, *Ends and Means* (London: Chatto &

NOTES

Windus, 1937), pp. 289–94; *The Perennial Philosophy* (London: Fontana Books, 1958, paperback), pp. 33–34, 287–88.

25. "Seven Meditations," *VWW*, p. 163; "Action and Contemplation," *VWW*, pp. 366–67.

26. *Perennial Philosophy*, pp. 108–109, 213–14.

27. "Seven Meditations," *VWW*, pp. 165, 169; *Perennial Philosophy*, p. 116.

28. *Time Must Have a Stop*, p. 105.

29. Aldous Huxley, *After Many a Summer* (London: Chatto & Windus, 1950), pp. 162–63, 165–66; "Words and Reality," *VWW*, p. 282.

30. *Perennial Philosophy*, pp. 192, 234, 246.

31. *Ibid.*, p. 197; *After Many a Summer*, pp. 105–110.

32. *Time Must Have a Stop*, pp. 295–98; see also *VVW*, pp. 209–211.

33. *Perennial Philosophy*, pp. 79, 146.

34. *Time Must Have a Stop*, pp. 138 ff., 302 ff.

35. Aldous Huxley, *The Devils of Loudun* (New York: Harper & Brothers, 1952), pp. 67, 69; "Seven Meditations," *VWW*, p. 168; *Perennial Philosophy*, pp. 79, 173.

CHAPTER 6. ZEN BUDDHISM

1. Bernard Phillips, ed., *The Essentials of Zen Buddhism, Selected from the Writings of Daisetz T. Suzuki* (New York: E. P. Dutton & Co., 1962), Introduction, p. xxxvi.

2. Soyen Shaku, *Sermons of a Buddhist Abbot: Addresses on Religious Subjects*, Daisetz Teitaro Suzuki, trans. (Chicago: Open Court Publishing Co., 1906). See also *Zen Notes* (leaflet published by the First Zen Institute of America), IV (November, 1957); Phillips, p. xxxvii; Clay Lancaster, *The Japanese Influence in America* (New York: Walton H. Rawls, 1963), p. 243.

3. Shaku, p. 128.

4. *Zen Notes; The First Zen Institute of America in Japan* (Kyoto: The First Zen Institute of America in Japan, 1959), pp.

1–2; *Cat's Yawn: A Zen Miscellany* (New York: The First Zen Institute of America, 1947); Lancaster, pp. 243, 263.

5. Oryu, *The Iron Flute*, Nyogen Senzaki and Ruth Strout McCandless, trans. and ed. (Rutland, Vt.: C. E. Tuttle Co., 1961), pp. 155 ff., gives biographical information on Nyogen Senzaki.

6. Phillips, pp. xxxvi–xil; Winthrop Sargeant, "Profiles: Great Simplicity," *New Yorker*, August 31, 1957, p. 48; see also Shaku, *Sermons*, Translator's Preface.

7. Phillips, pp. xxxvii–xil.

8. See, for example, his *Studies in Zen* (London: Rider & Co., 1955), pp. 74–84, 203.

9. Daisetz Teitaro Suzuki, *Essays in Zen Buddhism*, First Series (New York, Grove Press, 1961), pp. 60, 103–117, 163–228. For somewhat variant historical accounts see Heinrich Dumoulin, *A History of Zen Buddhism*, Paul Peachey, trans. (New York: Pantheon Books, 1963).

10. *Essays*, First Series, pp. 79, 318.

11. Daisetz Teitaro Suzuki, *Essays in Zen Buddhism*, Second Series (Boston: Beacon Press, 1952), pp. 84, 85.

12. *Ibid.*, pp. 85–89; Ruth Fuller Sasaki, *Zen: A Method for Religious Awakening* (Kyoto: The First Zen Institute of America in Japan, 1959), pp. 13, 20–22.

13. *Essays*, First Series, p. 230.

14. *Ibid.*, p. 263.

15. *Ibid.*, p. 240.

16. *Ibid.*, pp. 215, 245.

17. *Essays*, Second Series, pp. 28–34. Each of these numbered passages is an extract from a fuller discussion.

18. *Essays*, First Series, pp. 246–47, 260–61, 264–65.

19. Quoted in Alan W. Watts, *The Way of Zen* (New York: Mentor Books, 1959, paperback), pp. 33–34.

20. Daisetz Teitaro Suzuki, *The Training of the Zen Buddhist Monk* (New York: University Books., 1965), pp. xviii-xxii.

21. *Essays*, First Series, Editor's Foreword, p. 7.

22. *Ibid.*, p. 20.

23. *Ibid.*, p. 263.

24. See James Bissett Pratt, *The Pilgrimage of Buddhism and a Buddhist Pilgrimage* (New York: The Macmillan Co., 1928), pp. 237–41.

25. Daisetz Teitaro Suzuki, *Mysticism: Christian and Buddhist: the Eastern and Western Way* (New York: Collier Books, 1962, paperback), pp. 28, 29–30.

26. Beatrice Lane Suzuki, *Mahayana Buddhism* (London: Allen & Unwin, 1959), p. 93. On the Kegon view see also Daisetz Teitaro Suzuki, *The Essence of Buddhism* (Kyoto: Hozokan, 1948), pp. 51 ff.

27. Quotations from *Essays,* First Series, pp. 272, 273.

28. Suzuki, *Mysticism,* p. 20.

29. Daisetz Teitaro Suzuki, *Essays in Zen Buddhism,* Third Series (Kyoto: Eastern Buddhist Society, 1934), p. 335.

30. Alan W. Watts, *This Is It, and Other Essays on Zen and Spiritual Experience* (New York: Pantheon Books, 1960), pp. 29–31.

31. *Ibid.,* p. 31.

32. Alan W. Watts, *Behold the Spirit: A Study in the Necessity of Mystical Religion* (New York: Pantheon Books, 1947), p. 115; also *The Supreme Identity: An Essay on Oriental Metaphysic and the Christian Religion* (New York: Pantheon Books, 1950), p. 72, and *Beyond Theology: The Art of Godmanship* (New York: Pantheon Books, 1964), p. 204.

33. *This Is It,* pp. 34, 129, and *Psychotherapy East and West* (New York: Pantheon Books, 1961), p. 45. See also Watts's *The Wisdom of Insecurity* (New York: Pantheon Books, 1951), pp. 9–10, 135–52, and *Beyond Theology,* pp. 225–29.

34. *The Way of Zen,* pp. xi, xii, 158–59.

35. For more on this, see chap. 7 of this volume.

36. Alan W. Watts, "Beat Zen, Square Zen, and Zen," *Chicago Review,* XII (Summer, 1958), 3–11 (quotations from p. 11). For Kerouac's and Suzuki's statements, see Phillips, p. 373.

37. *Time,* May 26, 1958, p. 65.

38. Isshu Miura and Ruth Fuller Sasaki, *Zen Dust: The History of the Koan and Koan Study in Rinzai (Lin-Chi) Zen*

(New York: Harcourt, Brace & World, 1966), p. 27; Ruth Fuller Sasaki, *Zen: A Method*, p. 5.

39. Paul Wienpahl, *The Matter of Zen: A Brief Account of Zazen* (New York: New York University Press, 1964), pp. 139, 145.

40. Philip Kapleau, compiler, trans., and ed., *The Three Pillars of Zen: Teaching, Practice, and Enlightenment* (New York: Harper & Row, 1966), p. 208. See also Kapleau, " 'All is One, One is None, None Is All' " *New York Times Magazine*, March 6, 1966, pp. 26 ff.

41. Kapleau, *Three Pillars of Zen*, pp. 228, 229.

42. *Ibid.*, pp. xv, 16.

43. *Ibid.*, pp. 15, 21, 83, 84.

44. *Ibid.*, p. 204.

45. On Kapleau and the active Zen centers in 1969, see the periodical of the Zen Center of San Francisco, *Wind Bell*, VIII (Fall, 1969), 53 and *passim*. On Tassajara, see *Time*, October 18, 1968, p. 80.

CHAPTER 7. PSYCHOLOGY AND PSYCHEDELIC
EXPERIENCE

1. Editors' comment in Gardner and Lois B. Murphy, eds., *Asian Psychology* (New York: Basic Books, 1968), p. 96.

2. Swami Prabhavananda, *The Spiritual Heritage of India* (New York: Doubleday–Anchor Books, 1964, paperback). Quoted phrases from p. xxi.

3. Swami Akhilananda, *Hindu Psychology: Its Meaning for the West* (New York: Harper & Brothers, 1946), pp. 166–67, 169.

4. Swami Akhilananda, *Mental Health and Hindu Psychology* (2d ed.; London: George Allen & Unwin, 1952), p. xvi.

5. Daisetz Teitaro Suzuki, *Essays in Zen Buddhism*, First Series (New York: Grove Press, 1961), pp. 32, 251. Heinrich Dumoulin, in his *History of Zen Buddhism*, Paul Peachey, trans. (New York: Pantheon Books, 1963), suggests James's influence on Suzuki's theory of the unconscious (p. 278).

6. Daisetz Teitaro Suzuki, *The Zen Doctrine of No-Mind: The Significance of the Sutra of Hui-neng* (*Wei-Lang*) (2d ed.; London: Rider & Co., 1958), pp. 57, 120.

7. Daisetz Teitaro Suzuki, *An Introduction to Zen Buddhism* (Evergreen Black Cat ed.; New York: Grove Press, 1964, paperback), p. 22.

8. Daisetz Teitaro Suzuki, Erich Fromm, and Richard De Martino, *Zen Buddhism and Psychoanalysis* (New York: Harper & Brothers, 1960), p. 139.

9. *Ibid.*, p. 18; quoted in italics by Fromm on p. 131.

10. *Ibid.*, pp. 10, 16.

11. See his statement in *This Is My Faith: The Convictions of Representative Americans Today*, Stewart G. Cole, ed. (New York: Harper & Brothers, 1956), pp. 212–27.

12. Pitirim A. Sorokin, *The Ways and Power of Love: Types, Factors, and Techniques of Moral Transformation* (Boston: Beacon Press, 1954), pp. 83, 84, 98–100.

13. Thérèse Brosse, "Contribution to the Experimental Study of Altruism: Instrumental Explorations of Yoga Techniques," *Forms and Techniques of Altruistic and Spiritual Growth*, Pitirim A. Sorokin, ed. (Boston: Beacon Press, 1954), pp. 189–282, quotations from pp. 281, 282; Pitirim A. Sorokin, *A Long Journey: The Autobiography of Pitirim A. Sorokin* (New Haven: College & University Press, 1963), p. 289.

14. "Technique of Emotional Development and Integration," *Explorations in Altruistic Love and Behavior: A Symposium*, Pitirim A. Sorokin, ed. (Boston: Beacon Press, 1950), pp. 301–311.

15. Sorokin, *A Long Journey*, pp. 291–92.

16. Aldous Huxley, *The Doors of Perception* and *Heaven and Hell* (New York: Harper Colophon Books, 1963, paperback), pp. 12, 22, 17, 18, 41, 42–43, 66, 73, 76–78, 85–86, 156. Huxley consistently uses the spelling, "mescalin."

17. "Drugs that Shape Men's Minds," *Saturday Evening Post*, October 18, 1958, pp. 111, 113. For more restrained comment, see Aldous Huxley, *Brave New World Revisited* (New York: Harper & Brothers, 1958), chap. 8, "Chemical Persuasion."

18. Gerald Heard in *Aldous Huxley 1894–1963: A Memorial Volume*, Julian Huxley, ed. (London: Chatto & Windus, 1965), pp. 104–105.

19. Aldous Huxley, *Island* (New York: Harper & Brothers, 1962), *passim*, especially chap. 15.

20. *Ibid.*, p. 85; Laura Archera Huxley, *This Timeless Moment: A Personal View of Aldous Huxley* (New York: Farrar, Straus & Giroux, 1968), p. 176.

21. Quotations from Huxley's account, printed in Laura Huxley, *This Timeless Moment*, pp. 20–25.

22. *Ibid.*, pp. 131, 303–308.

23. Timothy Leary, "The Religious Experience: Its Production and Interpretation," *The Psychedelic Review*, I, No. 3 (1964), 324–46; also his *High Priest* (New York: World Publishing Co., 1968), pp. 64–67, 112 ff., 288.

24. The interview, which also gives biographical facts on Leary, is reprinted in Timothy Leary, *The Politics of Ecstasy* (New York: G. P. Putnam's Sons, 1968), pp. 118–59, quotation from p. 127. Compare Donald B. Louria, "The Abuse of LSD," in *LSD, Man & Society*, Richard C. DeBold and Russell C. Leaf, eds. (Middletown, Conn.: Wesleyan University Press, 1967), pp. 42–43, 49; and Louria, *The Drug Scene* (New York: McGraw-Hill Book Co., 1968), pp. 145–47.

25. See Theodore Roszak, *The Making of a Counter Culture: Reflections on the Technocratic Society and Its Youthful Opposition* (New York: Doubleday & Co., 1969), pp. 27, 32–33, 62–66; Frank Barron, "Motivational Patterns in LSD Usage," in DeBold and Leaf, eds., *LSD, Man & Society*, pp. 3–19; Louria, *Drug Scene*, pp. 15–45.

26. Louria, *Drug Scene*, pp. 10–11.

27. December 2, 1968, p. 20.

28. R. C. Zaehner, *Mysticism Sacred and Profane: An Inquiry into Some Varieties of Praeternatural Experience* (Oxford: Clarendon Press, 1957), pp. xv, 9. For a critique of Zaehner's argument, see Huston Smith, "Do Drugs Have Religious Import?" *Journal of Philosophy*, LXI (October 1, 1964), 517–30.

29. Alan W. Watts, *The Joyous Cosmology: Adventures in the Chemistry of Consciousness* (New York: Pantheon Books, 1962), p. 17; also his "Psychedelics and Religious Experience," in *The Religious Situation: 1969,* Donald R. Cutler, ed. (Boston: Beacon Press, 1969), p. 617.

30. For a brief summary of this experiment and others of a similar nature, see Walter N. Pahnke, "LSD and Religious Experience," in DeBold and Leaf, eds., *LSD, Man & Society,* pp. 60–84. For a more detailed summary of the Good Friday experiment, see Pahnke, "Drugs and Mysticism," *International Journal of Parapsychology,* VIII (Spring, 1966), 295–320.

31. Sidney Cohen, *The Beyond Within: The LSD Story* (New York: Atheneum, 1965), p. 102; R. E. L. Masters and Jean Houston, *The Varieties of Psychedelic Experience* (New York: Holt, Rinehart & Winston, 1966), p. 307.

32. Richard Blum and Associates, *Utopiates: The Use and Users of LSD-25* (New York: Atherton Press, 1964), p. 287.

33. Louria, *Drug Scene,* pp. 101–110, 147–61 (quotation from pp. 147–48), 169–73; *Newsweek,* August 18, 1969, p. 89; Roszak, p. 33; *The Press-Enterprise* (Riverside, Calif.), August 25, 1968, p. B–6.

34. Louria, *Drug Scene,* pp. 161–63; Neil L. Chayet, "Social and Legal Aspects of LSD Usage," in DeBold and Leaf, eds., *LSD, Man & Society,* pp. 92–124; Cohen, p. 220.

35. Leary, *High Priest,* pp. 290, 292, 310.

36. Walter Houston Clark, "The Mystical Consciousness and World Understanding," *Journal for the Scientific Study of Religion,* IV (Spring, 1965), 159.

37. Walter Houston Clark, *Chemical Ecstasy: Psychedelic Drugs and Religion* (New York: Sheed & Ward, 1969), pp. v-vi, 54–56, 129, 155, 157.

38. Gerald Heard, *The Five Ages of Man: The Psychology of Human History* (New York: The Julian Press, 1963), pp. 236–41; see also Heard, "Can This Drug Enlarge Man's Mind?" *The Psychedelic Review,* I (June, 1963), 7–17.

39. Jane Dunlap (pseudonym), *Exploring Inner Space: Per-*

sonal Experiences under LSD-25 (New York: Harcourt, Brace & World, 1961), p. 15.

40. All quotations are from Ralph Metzner, ed., *The Ecstatic Adventure* (New York: The Macmillan Co., 1968), pp. 78–83.

41. Quoted by Clark in his *Chemical Ecstasy*, p. 18.

42. Alan W. Watts, *Nature, Man and Woman* (New York: Pantheon Books, 1958), p. 78, *n.* 11.

CHAPTER 8. THE MYSTICAL STRAND

1. Rufus Jones, *Some Exponents of Mystical Religion* (New York: Abingdon Press, 1930), pp. 209, 212.

2. Rudolf Otto, *The Idea of the Holy: An Inquiry into the Non-Rational Factor in the Idea of the Divine and Its Relation to the Rational,* John W. Harvey, trans. (rev. ed.; London: Humphrey Milford and Oxford University Press, 1931), p. 22.

3. For an informative, unsympathetic survey of those established before 1930, see Wendell Thomas, *Hinduism Invades America* (New York: Beacon Press, 1930).

4. See Paramhansa (variant spelling on title page) Yogananda, *Autobiography of a Yogi* (7th ed.; Los Angeles: Self-Realization Fellowship, 1956), p. 357; and *Self-Realization Magazine,* XL (January-March, 1969), pp. 43–48.

5. John Tracy Ellis, *American Catholicism* (Chicago: University of Chicago Press, 1956, paperback), p. 133; *Time,* February 9, 1968, p. 66.

6. William Hedgepeth, "The Non-Drug Turn-On Hits Campus," *Look,* February 6, 1968, pp. 68–78; *The Press* (Riverside, Calif.), August 12, 1968, p. A-15. See also Maharishi Mahesh Yogi, *The Science of Being and Art of Living* (New York: New American Library, 1968).

7. February 9, 1968, pp. 52–59.

8. See Martin E. Marty, "The Religious Situation: An Introduction," in *The Religious Situation: 1968,* Donald R. Cutler, ed. (Boston: Beacon Press, 1968), pp. xxi-xlvii, and Harvey Cox, *The Secular City: Secularization and Urbanization in Theologi-*

cal Perspective (rev. ed.; New York: The Macmillan Co., 1966). For perspective on the "death of God" argument see Edwin Scott Gaustad, ed., *Religious Issues in American History* (New York: Harper Forum Books, 1968, paperback), pp. 272–94.

9. Rufus Jones, *Some Exponents of Mystical Religion*, p. 224.

Bibliography

This list is restricted to sources cited in the text and notes.

BOOKS AND PAMPHLETS

ADDISON, CHARLES MORRIS. *The Theory and Practice of Mysticism.* New York: E. P. Dutton & Co., 1918.

AKHILANANDA, SWAMI. *Hindu Psychology: Its Meaning for the West.* New York: Harper & Brothers, 1946.

———. *Hindu View of Christ.* New York: Philosophical Library, 1949.

———. *Mental Health and Hindu Psychology.* 2d ed. London: George Allen & Unwin, 1952.

ALLEN, GAY WILSON. *William James: A Biography.* New York: Viking Press, 1967.

AMES, VAN METER. *Zen and American Thought.* Honolulu: University of Hawaii Press, 1962.

ATZBAUGH, WILLIAM. *Seek Ye the Christ.* San Gabriel, Calif.: Willing Publishing Co., 1949.

AUGUSTINUS, ST. AURELIUS. *The Confessions of St. Augustine.* Translated by E. B. Pusey. New York: E. P. Dutton & Co., 1951.

BENNETT, CHARLES A. *The Dilemma of Religious Knowledge.* New Haven: Yale University Press, 1931.

————. *A Philosophical Study of Mysticism.* New Haven: Yale University Press, 1931.

BENNETT, LERONE, JR. *What Manner of Man: A Biography of Martin Luther King, Jr.* Chicago: Johnson Publishing Co., 1964.

BLAKE, WILLIAM. *The Complete Writings.* Edited by Geoffrey Keynes. London: Nonesuch Press, 1957.

BLOOD, BENJAMIN PAUL. *The Anaesthetic Revelation and the Gist of Philosophy.* Amsterdam, N. Y.: Privately printed, 1874.

————. *Pluriverse: An Essay in the Philosophy of Pluralism.* London: Kegan Paul, Trench, Trubner & Co., 1920.

BLUM, RICHARD, AND ASSOCIATES. *Utopiates: The Use and Users of LSD-25.* New York: Atherton Press, 1964.

BRINTON, HOWARD HAINES. *Friends for 300 Years: The History and Beliefs of the Society of Friends since George Fox Started the Quaker Movement.* New York: Harper & Brothers, 1952.

BUBER, MARTIN. *Hasidism and Modern Man.* Edited and translated by Maurice Friedman. New York: Horizon Press, 1958.

BUCKE, RICHARD MAURICE. *Cosmic Consciousness: A Study in the Evolution of the Human Mind.* New York: E. P. Dutton & Co., 1923.

BUCKHAM, JOHN WRIGHT. *Mysticism and Modern Life.* New York: The Abingdon Press, 1915.

Cat's Yawn: A Zen Miscellany. New York: The First Zen Institute of America, 1947.

CHRISTY, ARTHUR. *The Orient in American Transcendentalism.* New York: Columbia University Press, 1932.

CLARK, WALTER HOUSTON. *Chemical Ecstasy: Psychedelic Drugs and Religion.* New York: Sheed & Ward, 1969.

COHEN, SIDNEY. *The Beyond Within: The LSD Story.* New York: Atheneum, 1965.

COLE, STEWART G., ed. *This Is My Faith: The Convictions of Representative Americans Today.* New York: Harper & Brothers, 1956.

COX, HARVEY. *The Secular City: Secularization and Urbaniza-*

tion in Theological Perspective. Rev. ed. New York: The Macmillan Co., 1966.

CURTI, Merle. *The Growth of American Thought.* 3d ed. New York: Harper & Row, 1964.

CUTLER, DONALD R., ed. *The Religious Situation: 1968.* Boston: Beacon Press, 1968.

————, ed. *The Religious Situation: 1969.* Boston: Beacon Press, 1969.

DeBOLD, RICHARD C., AND LEAF, RUSSELL C., eds. *LSD, Man & Society.* Middletown, Conn.: Wesleyan University Press, 1967.

DUMOULIN, HEINRICH. *A History of Zen Buddhism.* Translated from the German by Paul Peachey. New York: Pantheon Books, 1963.

DUNLAP, JANE [pseud.]. *Exploring Inner Space: Personal Experience under LSD-25.* New York: Harcourt, Brace & World, 1961.

ECKHART, MEISTER. *Meister Eckhart.* Translated by Raymond Bernard Blakney. New York: Harper Torchbooks, 1957, paperback.

ELIADE, Mircea. *Yoga: Immortality and Freedom.* Translated from the French by Willard R. Trask. New York: Pantheon Books, 1958.

ELIOT, SIR CHARLES. *Hinduism and Buddhism: An Historical Sketch.* Vol. 2. London: Routledge & Kegan Paul, 1921.

ELLIS, JOHN TRACY. *American Catholicism.* Chicago: University of Chicago Press, 1956, paperback.

FERM, VERGILIUS, ed. *Contemporary American Theology: Theological Autobiographies.* Vol. 1. New York: Round Table Press, 1932.

FINKELSTEIN, LOUIS, ed. *The Jews, Their History, Culture, and Religion.* Vol. 2. New York: Harper & Brothers, 1960.

The First Zen Institute of America in Japan. Kyoto: The First Zen Institute of America in Japan, 1959.

FREUD, SIGMUND. *The Complete Psychological Works.* Translated from the German under the general editorship of James

MAY, HENRY F. *The End of American Innocence: A Study of the First Years of Our Own Time 1912–1917.* New York: Alfred A. Knopf, 1959.

MERTON, THOMAS. *The Ascent to Truth.* New York: Harcourt, Brace & Co., 1951.

―――. *The Living Bread.* New York: Farrar, Straus & Cudahy, 1956.

―――. *Mystics and Zen Masters.* New York: Farrar, Straus & Giroux, 1967.

―――. *New Seeds of Contemplation.* Norfolk, Conn.: New Directions, 1961.

―――. *No Man Is an Island.* New York: Harcourt, Brace & Co., 1955.

―――. *Seeds of Contemplation.* Norfolk, Conn.: New Directions, 1949.

―――. *Selected Poems.* Enlarged ed. New York: New Directions, 1967, paperback.

―――. *The Seven Storey Mountain.* New York: Signet Books, 1952, paperback.

―――. *The Sign of Jonas.* New York: Harcourt, Brace & Co., 1953.

―――. *The Silent Life.* New York: Farrar, Straus & Cudahy, 1957.

―――. *Thoughts in Solitude.* New York: Farrar, Straus & Cudahy, 1958.

―――. *The Waters of Siloe.* New York: Harcourt, Brace & Co., 1949.

METZNER, RALPH, ed. *The Ecstatic Adventure.* New York: The Macmillan Co., 1968.

MIURA, ISSHU, and SASAKI, RUTH FULLER. *Zen Dust: The History of the Koan and Koan Study in Rinzai (Lin-Chi) Zen.* New York: Harcourt, Brace & World, 1966.

MONTAGUE, MARGARET PRESCOTT. *Twenty Minutes of Reality.* Saint Paul, Minn.: Macalester Park Publishing Co., 1947.

MURPHY, GARDNER, and MURPHY, LOIS B., eds. *Asian Psychology.* New York: Basic Books, 1968.

NIKHILANANDA, SWAMI. *Hinduism: Its Meaning for the Libera-*

tion of the Spirit. New York: Harper & Brothers, 1958.
―――. *Vivekananda, A Biography.* New York: Ramakrishna-Vivekananda Center, 1953.

ORYU. *The Iron Flute.* Translated and edited by Nyogen Senzaki and Ruth Strout McCandless. Rutland, Vt.: C. E. Tuttle Co., 1961.

OTTO, RUDOLF. *The Idea of the Holy: An Inquiry into the Non-Rational Factor in the Idea of the Divine and Its Relation to the Rational.* Translated by John W. Harvey. Rev. and enlarged ed. London: Humphrey Milford and Oxford University Press, 1931.

―――. *Mysticism East and West: A Comparative Analysis of the Nature of Mysticism.* Translated by Bertha L. Bracey and Richenda C. Payne. New York: Collier Books, 1962, paperback.

PERRY, RALPH BARTON. *The Thought and Character of William James.* Vol. 2. Boston: Little & Brown & Co., 1935.

PHILLIPS, BERNARD, ed. *The Essentials of Zen Buddhism, Selected from the Writings of Daisetz T. Suzuki.* New York: E. P. Dutton & Co., 1962.

PLOTINUS. *The Enneads.* Translation by Stephen MacKenna revised by B. S. Page. 3d ed. London: Faber & Faber, 1962.

PRABHAVANANDA, SWAMI. *The Sermon on the Mount according to Vedanta.* Hollywood: Vedanta Press, 1964.

―――. *The Spiritual Heritage of India.* New York: Doubleday–Anchor Books, 1964, paperback.

PRATT, JAMES BISSETT. *The Pilgrimage of Buddhism and a Buddhist Pilgrimage.* New York: The Macmillan Co., 1928.

―――. *The Religious Consciousness: A Psychological Study.* New York: The Macmillan Co., 1920.

RADHAKRISHNAN, SARVEPALLI. *Indian Philosophy.* Vol. 2. Rev. 2d ed. New York: The Macmillan Co., 1931.

REPS, PAUL, compiler. *Zen Flesh, Zen Bones: A Collection of Zen & Pre-Zen Writings.* Rutland, Vt.: Charles E. Tuttle Co., 1957.

ROSZAK, THEODORE. *The Making of a Counter Culture: Reflec-*

tions on the Technocratic Society and Its Youthful Opposition.
New York: Doubleday & Co., 1969.

ROYCE, JOSIAH. *The World and the Individual.* 2 vols. New
York: The Macmillan Co., 1901.

RUSSELL, BERTRAND. *Mysticism and Logic and other Essays.*
London: George Allen & Unwin, 1917.

SANTAYANA, GEORGE. *The Life of Reason.* Vol. 3: *Reason in
Religion.* New York: Charles Scribner's Sons, 1905.

SASAKI, RUTH FULLER. *Zen: A Method for Religious Awakening.* Kyoto: First Zen Institute of America in Japan, 1959.

————. *Zen: A Religion.* New York: First Zen Institute of
America, 1958.

SCHNEIDER, HERBERT WALLACE. *Religion in 20th Century
America.* Rev. ed. New York: Atheneum, 1964, paperback.

SCHOLEM, GERSHOM G. *Major Trends in Jewish Mysticism.* 3d
rev. ed. New York: Shocken Books, 1954.

SHAKU, SOYEN. *Sermons of a Buddhist Abbot: Addresses on
Religious Subjects.* Translated by Daisetz Teitaro Suzuki.
Chicago: Open Court Publishing Co., 1906.

SMITH, JAMES WARD, and JAMISON, A. LELAND, eds. *Religion
in American Life.* 3 vols. Princeton: Princeton University
Press, 1961.

SMITH, MARGARET, trans. and ed. *Readings from the Mystics of
Islam.* London: Luzac & Co., 1950.

SOROKIN, PITIRIM A. *A Long Journey: The Autobiography of
Pitirim A. Sorokin.* New Haven: College and University
Press, 1963.

————. *The Ways and Power of Love: Types, Factors, and Techniques of Moral Transformation.* Boston: Beacon Press, 1954.

————, ed. *Explorations in Altruistic Love and Behavior: A Symposium.* Boston: Beacon Press, 1950.

————, ed. *Forms and Techniques of Altruistic and Spiritual
Growth.* Boston: Beacon Press, 1954.

SPILLER, ROBERT E. and OTHERS, eds. *Literary History of the
United States.* 2 vols. 3d ed. rev. New York: The Macmillan
Co., 1963.

185

STACE, W. T. *Mysticism and Philosophy.* Philadelphia: J. B. Lippincott Co., 1960.

———. *The Teachings of the Mystics.* New York: Mentor Books, 1960, paperback.

STIERNOTTE, ALFRED P., ed., *Mysticism and the Modern Mind.* New York: Liberal Arts Press, 1959.

SUZUKI, BEATRICE LANE. *Mahayana Buddhism.* London: Allen & Unwin, 1959.

SUZUKI, DAISETZ TEITARO. *Essays in Zen Buddhism.* First Series: New York, Grove Press, 1961. Second Series: Boston, Beacon Press, 1952. Third Series: Kyoto, Eastern Buddhist Society, 1934.

———. *The Essence of Buddhism.* Kyoto: Hozokan, 1948.

———. *An Introduction to Zen Buddhism.* Evergreen Black Cat ed. New York: Grove Press, 1964, paperback.

———. *Manual of Zen Buddhism.* New York: Grove Press, 1960.

———. *Mysticism: Christian and Buddhist: The Eastern and Western Way.* New York: Collier Books, 1962, paperback.

———. *Studies in the Lankavatara Sutra, One of the Most Important Texts of Mahayana Buddhism, in Which Almost All Its Principle Tenets Are Presented, including the Teaching of Zen.* London: Routledge, 1930.

———. *Studies in Zen.* London: Rider & Co., 1955.

———. *The Training of the Zen Buddhist Monk.* New York: University Books, 1965.

———. *Zen Buddhism and Its Influence on Japanese Culture.* Kyoto: Eastern Buddhist Society, 1938.

———. *The Zen Doctrine of No-Mind: The Significance of the Sutra of Hui-neng (Wei-Lang).* 2d ed. London: Rider & Co., 1958.

———, FROMM, ERICH, and DE MARTINO, RICHARD. *Zen Buddhism and Psychoanalysis.* New York: Harper & Brothers, 1960.

THOMAS, WENDELL. *Hinduism Invades America.* New York: Beacon Press, 1930.

THURMAN, HOWARD. *The Creative Encounter: An Interpretation of Religion and the Social Witness.* New York: Harper & Brothers, 1954.

———. *Deep Is the Hunger: Meditations for Apostles of Sensitiveness.* New York: Harper & Brothers, 1951.

———. *Disciplines of the Spirit.* New York: Harper & Row, 1963.

———. *Footprints of a Dream: The Story of the Church for the Fellowship of All Peoples.* New York, Harper & Brothers, 1959.

———. *The Growing Edge.* New York: Harper & Brothers, 1956.

———. *The Inward Journey.* New York: Harper & Brothers, 1961.

———. *Jesus and the Disinherited.* New York: Abingdon-Cokesbury Press, 1949.

———. *The Luminous Darkness: A Personal Interpretation of the Anatomy of Segregation and the Ground of Hope.* New York: Harper & Row, 1965.

———. *Meditations of the Heart.* New York: Harper & Brothers, 1953.

———. *Mysticism and the Experience of Love.* Wallingford, Pa.: Pendle Hill, 1961.

UNDERHILL, EVELYN. *Mysticism: A Study in the Nature and Development of Man's Spiritual Consciousness.* 12th ed. New York: Meridian Books, 1955, paperback.

VINING, ELIZABETH GRAY. *Rufus Jones, Friend of Life.* Philadelphia: J. B. Lippincott Co., 1958.

WATTS, ALAN W. *Behold the Spirit: A Study in the Necessity of Mystical Religion.* New York: Pantheon Books, 1947.

———. *Beyond Theology: The Art of Godmanship.* New York: Pantheon Books, 1964.

———. *The Joyous Cosmology: Adventures in the Chemistry of Consciousness.* New York, Pantheon Books, 1962.

———. *Nature, Man and Woman.* New York: Pantheon Books, 1958.

———. *Psychotherapy East and West.* New York: Pantheon Books, 1961.

————. *The Spirit of Zen: A Way of Life, Work and Art in the Far East.* London: John Murray, 1936.

————. *The Supreme Identity: An Essay on Oriental Metaphysic and the Christian Religion.* New York: Pantheon Books, 1950.

————. *This Is It, and Other Essays on Zen and Spiritual Experience.* New York: Pantheon Books, 1960.

————. *The Way of Zen.* New York: Mentor Books, 1959, paperback.

————. *The Wisdom of Insecurity.* New York: Pantheon Books, 1951.

WIEMAN, HENRY NELSON, and MELAND, BERNARD EUGENE. *American Philosophies of Religion.* Chicago: Willett, Clark & Company, 1936.

WIENPAHL, PAUL. *The Matter of Zen: A Brief Account of Zazen.* New York: New York University Press, 1964.

YATES, ELIZABETH. *Howard Thurman: Portrait of a Practical Dreamer.* New York: John Day Co., 1964.

YOGANANDA, PARAMHANSA (variant spelling on title page). *Autobiography of a Yogi.* 7th ed. Los Angeles: Self-Realization Fellowship, 1956.

ZAEHNER, R. C. *Mysticism Sacred and Profane: An Inquiry into Some Varieties of Praeternatural Experience.* Oxford: Clarendon Press, 1957.

OTHER SOURCES

CHERBONNIER, E. LaB. "A. J. Heschel and the Philosophy of the Bible: Mystic or Rationalist?" *Commentary,* XXVII (January, 1959), 23–29.

CLARK, WALTER HOUSTON. "The Mystical Consciousness and World Understanding." *Journal for the Scientific Study of Religion,* IV (Spring, 1965), 152–61.

HEARD, GERALD. "Can This Drug Enlarge Man's Mind?" *The Psychedelic Review,* I (June, 1963) 7–17.

HEDGEPETH, WILLIAM. "The Non-Drug Turn-On Hits Campus." *Look,* February 6, 1968, pp. 68–78.

Bibliography

HUXLEY, ALDOUS. "Drugs that Shape Men's Minds." *The Saturday Evening Post,* October 18, 1958, pp. 111, 113.

JAMES, WILLIAM. "A Suggestion about Mysticism." *Journal of Philosophy,* VII (February 17, 1910), 85–92.

KAPLEAU, PHILIP. " 'All Is One, One Is None, None Is All.' " *The New York Times Magazine,* March 6, 1966, pp. 26–27, 78, 80–81, 84.

LEARY, TIMOTHY. "The Religious Experience: Its Production and Interpretation." *The Psychedelic Review,* I (No. 3, 1964), 324–346.

Newsweek. December 2, 1968, p. 20. August 18, 1969, p. 89.

PAHNKE, WALTER N. "Drugs and Mysticism." *International Journal of Parapsychology,* VIII (Spring, 1966), 295–320.

PETUCHOWSKI, JACOB J. "Faith as the Leap of Action: The Theology of Abraham Joshua Heschel." *Commentary,* XXV (May, 1958), 390–97.

The Press (Riverside, Calif.). August 12, 1968, p. A-15.

The Press-Enterprise (Riverside, Calif.). August 25, 1968, p. B-6.

SARGEANT, WINTHROP. "Profiles: Great Simplicity." *The New Yorker,* August 31, 1957, pp. 34–51.

Self-Realization Magazine, XL (January-March, 1969), 43–48.

SMITH, HUSTON. "Do Drugs Have Religious Import?" *The Journal of Philosophy,* LXI (October 1, 1964), 517–530.

Time. May 26, 1958, p. 65. February 9, 1968, p. 66. October 18, 1968, p. 80.

WATTS, ALAN W. "Beat Zen, Square Zen, and Zen." *Chicago Review,* XII (Summer, 1958), 3–11.

"Year of the Guru." *Life,* February 9, 1968, pp. 52–59.

Zen Notes (leaflet published by The First Zen Institute of America), IV (November, 1957), no paging.

NOTE: *For full roster of works quoted or cited in this volume from each person studied, see text, Notes, and Bibliography.*—ED.

191

Index

Lawrence, Brother, 41, 48
Lawrence, D. H., "life-worship" doctrine of, 87
Leary, Timothy, and LSD, 130–31; and psilocybin, 130, 132, 134; psychedelic experiments at Harvard, 130–31, 134; way of life of, 131, 133, 142; writings and statements of, 131, 139, 142
Leuba, James, *The Psychology of Religious Mysticism,* 31, 120
Light, 70; absolutely above our nature, 7; "blinding and neutralizing," 67–68; Clear Light of the Void, 88, 94; "a dazzling stream of illumination," 116; the divine, in man, 62; a flash of "overpowering brilliance," 62; God is, 5; infinite rays of, in Supreme Reality, 107; of the order of love, 67–68; the unchangeable, 5; "vivid sensation of lightness and clarity," 110; *See also* Inner Light
Limits and purpose of this study, ix–x, 2, 4, 7–8; "in the spirit of William James," 18
Limits of reason or mental process, 25, 45, 63, 64, 67, 71–72
Logical concepts, *see* Reason
Lord's Prayer, Huxley's invocation to the, 89; ladder to mystical perfection, 84; meaning of "evil" in the, 84–85
Lotze, Hermann, 41
Louria, Dr. Donald B., 131, 132; dangers in use of drugs, 135–36; *The Drug Scene,* 127, 135–36
Love, or *agape,* 30, 34, 70; the amazing bondedness of divine, 48; central concept of Merton's thought, 70; direct contact with Truth has the nature of, 67–68; empties the soul of all pride, 71; of enemy, 57; God is, 90; God's invading, 48; for God and man and every living thing, 5; is the heart of mystical union, 70–72; and law, 90–91; leaves nothing but pure capacity for God, 71; "like swimming in the heart of the sun," 70; the man who knows Oneness with God lives in, 122; meaning of, 91; nature of, 57; peace and joy in divine, 72; prayer out of sheer, 54; the Way is of humility and, 89; "what Christianity might mean" by God's, 110

LSD, 125–27, 129–42, 151; abstention from, 147–48; brings either psychotic or visionary state, 134
Luther, Martin, 35

Magic, 6, 21
Maharishi Mahesh Yogi, guru, 147
Mahayana Buddhism, all Buddhas one in, 108; notion of Emptiness, 107; philosophic background of Zen, 110; religion of the Bodhisattva, 108; Zen Buddhism a sect of, 100
Man, all men are members of one another, 60; finite-infinite nature of, 30, 36, 37, 71; God, and universe one total whole, 114–15; must find his real Self, 74; relation of God to, 31; temple of divine spirit, 24; true end of, 74–75, 89, 111
Marguerite Marie, St., 31
Marijuana, 132, 135, 136, 147–48
Marks of mystical experience, authoritativeness, 103, 110; chief traits of satori, 103–04; direct, unitive experience of God, 4; faith, self-discipline, detachment, loss of ego, 79; a "fifth mark," 43; insight vs. analytic knowledge, 73; moral preparation for mystical life, 2; selflessness, 4; sense of oneness, 3; William James's four, 14, 43, 62–63
Mary, St., mother of Jesus, 79, 80
Masters, R. E. L., and Jean Houston, *Varieties of Psychedelic Experience,* 134–35, 139

199